ANNE WALLACE
P.O. BOX 163
SAN YGNACIO, TX 78067

PERSECUTION BY PROXY

The Civil Patrols in Guatamala

WRITTEN BY
Alice Jay

AND EDITED BY
Kerry Kennedy Cuomo
Helet Merkling
and
Nan Richardson

THE ROBERT F. KENNEDY MEMORIAL CENTER FOR HUMAN RIGHTS

Copyright 1993 by the Robert F. Kennedy
Memorial Center for Human Rights
All rights reserved

ISBN 1-881055-02-7

Photos by Vince Heptig and Chuck Olin

Cover photo of a young boy watching civil patrollers in Nebaj, Guatamala by Vince Heptig.

Additional copies of this report may be obtained free of charge from:

The Robert F. Kennedy Memorial Center for Human Rights
12 East 33rd Street
7th Floor
New York, N.Y. 10016
Tel. (212) 679-4120
Fax (212) 679-2517

Printed in the United States of America

"Everything that makes man's life worthwhile—family, work, education, a place to rear one's children and a place to rest one's head—all this depends on decisions of government; all can be swept away by a government which does not heed the demands of its people. Therefore, the essential humanity of men can be protected and preserved only where government must answer - not just to the wealthy; not just to those of a particular religion, or a particular race; but to all its people. And even government by the consent of the governed . . . must be limited in its power to act against its people; so that there may be no interference with the right to worship, or with the security of the home; no arbitrary imposition of pains or penalties by officials high or low; no restriction on the freedom of men to seek education or work or opportunity of any kind, so that each man may become all he is capable of becoming."

— *Robert F. Kennedy, 1966*
Cape Town, South Africa

ACKNOWLEDGEMENTS

This report was written by Alice Jay who has worked with CERJ and Amilcar Mendez Urizar during the last two years in Guatemala. Jill Wrigley wrote an initial draft of the report.

Kerry Kennedy Cuomo and Helet Merkling edited the report with Nan Richardson from Umbra Editions.

The Robert F. Kennedy Memorial Center for Human Rights wishes to express its sincere appreciation to everyone who helped to make this report possible; all the citizens of Guatamala who work for peace and respect for human rights; to Francisco Aguilar, Peter Barwick, Janos Fodor, Anna Gallagher, Vince Heptig, Andrew Kaufman, The Center for Human Rights Legal Action, Anne Manuel, Amilcar Mendez Urizar and members of CERJ, Karen Musalo, Chuck Olin, Elliot Schrage, and Bonnie Tenneriello for their help and insight; Gerry Leeds and Steve Grande for their assistance in printing this book.

The author wishes to thank The Stitchling European Human Rights Foundation for their support during 1991 and 1992 during which time the research for this report was conducted.

INDEX

I. PREFACE... 5

II. INTRODUCTION 8
   1. Overview... 8
   2. History of Guatemala................................... 11
   3. Human rights obligations of the Guatemalan Government 14

III. THE CIVIL PATROLS CONTROL THE PEOPLE............... 17
   1. The military created the civil patrols 17
   2. Indigenous men were forced to patrol 17
   3. Men who did not patrol were punished 18
   4. The military trained civil patrollers to control their communities and eliminate the opposition............................. 18
   5. Civil patrollers operated in combat 20
   6. The military extorted free labor from civil patrollers 20
   7. The military supervised civil patrol activities................ 20
   8. Conclusions: the military forced indigenous men to serve as instruments of its counterinsurgency strategy and to consolidate military domination of rural communities 21

IV. THE CIVIL PATROLS VIOLATE HUMAN RIGHTS 22
   1. Civil patrols maintain power over the indigenous people 22
      a. The civil patrollers force indigenous men to participate in the patrols... 23
      b. Non-patrollers are assassinated......................... 23
      c. Civil patrollers threaten and intimidate non-patrollers 24
      d. Civil patrollers shoot and beat non-patrollers.............. 25
      e. Civil patrollers discriminate against non-patrollers in community projects 26
      f. Minors are forced to patrol............................ 26
      g. Sanctions are imposed against patrollers who miss civil patrol duty 27
   2. The civil patrols attack organizations like CERJ which oppose the civil patrol system... 27
      a. CERJ members are assassinated........................ 27
      b. CERJ members are disappeared 28
      c. CERJ members are threatened......................... 29
   3. The civil patrols wield unconstitutional authority in communities... 29
      a. Illegal arrests 30
      b. Illegal forced labor................................... 31
      c. Control of freedom of movement....................... 31
   4. Conclusions: the civil patrols are not voluntary neighborhood watch groups, but serve to entrench control of the indigenous population in the Guatemalan highlands and attack human rights organizations which oppose the civil patrol system........................... 31

V. MILITARY IS RESPONSIBLE FOR THE CIVIL PATROLS ... 32
1. The military asserts that the civil patrols are independent, voluntary groups, denies military accountability for the patfols and denies that civil patrollers commit human rights abuses 32
2. The military is reponsible for the civil patrols and their actions 32
   a. The military arms the civil patrols 33
   b. The military is legally responsible for the civil patrols 33
   c. The military is organizationally responsible for the civil patrols . 33
3. The military compels indigenous men to perform civil patrol duty .. 34
   a. Army officials assert that the civil patrol service is obligatory .. 35
   b. Army officials intimidate those who wish to withdraw from patrolling.. 35
   c. Army officials threaten and detain those who have ceased patrolling 36
   d. The army discriminates against non-patrollers in military conscription 37
4. The military represses human rights organizations 38
   a. The military conducts a disinformation campaign against CERJ. 38
   b. The military attacks Amilcar Mendez Urizar................ 39
5. Conclusions: the military is legally responsible for the civil patrols which control by proxy the indigenous communities in the rural areas of Guatemala 41

VI. THE GOVERNMENT IS RESPONSIBLE FOR THE CIVIL PATROLS AND FOR HUMAN RIGHTS ABUSES............. 42
1. President Serrano promises reform and to uphold human rights.... 42
2. President Serrano accuses Amilcar Mendez Urizar of working with the insurgency... 42
3. The Government tolerates human rights violations 43
   a. The Government human rights institutions fail to adequately protect human rights 43
   b. The Government tolerates "paramilitary" intimidation against Amilcar Mendez and CERJ 45
      i. Assaults against Mendez............................. 45
      ii. Written death threats to Mendez 45
      iii. Circulation of defamatory material against Mendez and CERJ 46
4. The administration of justice in the highlands of Guatemala has failed 47
   a. The judiciary fails to protect human rights 48
      i. The *habeas corpus* remedy fails 48
      ii. Assassinations are not investigated 49
   b. The judicial system is flawed 51
   c. Civil patrols are the dominant rural authority.............. 53
   d. The civil patrols supersede the justice system 54
   e. The civil patrollers interfere with judicial proceedings 55

  i. Witnesses and victims are persecuted................ 55
  ii. Judges are threatened............................. 56
  iii. The military, not the police, enforces internal security 57
  iv. The police fail to investigate human rights abuses 58
 f. Chunima: a case study of the failure of the administration
  of justice...................................... 58
 g. Conclusions..................................... 63

VII. CONCLUSIONS 65

1. The Civil Patrols.................................. 65
2. The Military..................................... 65
3. The Civil Government 66

VIII. RECOMMENDATIONS............................. 67

1. The Guatemalan Goverment.......................... 67
2. The U.S. Government............................... 69
3. The International Community......................... 71

I. PREFACE

This report follows a mission to Guatemala by the Robert F. Kennedy Memorial Center for Human Rights ("RFK Center") from June 12-16, 1992. Members of the delegation included six attorneys: Francisco Aguilar, member of the U.N. Human Rights Committee and of the Arias Foundation; Kerry Kennedy Cuomo, Executive Director of the RFK Center; Dr. Janos Fodor, member of the U.N. Human Rights Committee and Hungarian Consul General to the United Nations; Helet Merkling, Program Director of the RFK Center; Elliot Schrage and Jill Wrigley, consultants to the RFK Center.

Prior to the mission, the delegation met with members of the U.S. Department of State and human rights monitors in Washington D.C. to discuss the current situation in Guatemala. During the mission in Guatemala, the delegation met with a wide range of individuals and organizations, including Guatemalan government officials, officers from the Guatemalan Armed Forces, representatives from the U.S. Embassy, nongovernmental human rights organizations, labor groups, student groups, and clergy from the Catholic Church. Government officials included Vice President Gustavo Espina Salguero; Fernando Hurtado Prem (then Minister of the Interior); Acisclo Valladares (then Attorney General); Bernardo Neumann, President of the Executive Commission for Human Rights ("COPREDEH"), and several other COPREDEH members. The delegation also met with senior military officers, including Jose Garcia Domingo Samayoa (Minister of Defense), Colonel Mario Rolando Terrazzo Pinot (military commander of Base No. 20 in the Quiche Province) and Captain Julio Alberto Yon Rivera (Director of the Department of Information of the Armed Forces). A meeting was held with Maria Eugenia de Sierra, the Deputy Procurator of the Office of the Human Rights Ombudsman.

The delegation also met with Amilcar Mendez Urizar, the recipient of the 1990 Robert F. Kennedy Human Rights Award, and with representatives from the Council for Ethnic Communities Runujel Junam/"We are all equal" ("CERJ"). CERJ is a community-based human rights organization founded by a group of indigenous peasants and Amilcar Mendez in July 1988 to monitor and promote fundamental freedoms and human rights. CERJ educates members of the indigenous communities in the highlands of Guatemala about their constitutional, human, and cultural rights. CERJ has suffered relentless repression and intimidation from the military and their subordinates, the civil patrols.

The delegation interviewed members of the National Council of Guatemalan Widows ("CONAVIGUA"); the Mutual Support Group for relatives of the Disappeared ("GAM"); the Civilian Populations in Resistance ("CPR"); the Center for the Investigation, Study and Protection of Human Rights ("CIEPRODH"); the National Council of the Displaced ("CONDEG"); the Committee of Peasant Unity ("CUC"); and the labor union umbrella group, the Unity of Syndical and Popular Action ("UASP"). A meeting was also held with the Bishop of Quiche, Monsignor Julio Cabrera. The delegation interviewed many victims of human rights abuses and family members who have lost loved ones in the struggle for human rights.

The primary purpose of the mission was to examine the human rights situation in Guatemala and its particular effects on Amilcar Mendez and members of CERJ. Discussions with government officials centered on the continuing military and governmental persecution of Mendez and members of CERJ; the current and future status of the civil patrols; the human rights violations committed by members of the civil patrols and the military against CERJ members and against non-patrollers; the impunity of human rights violators and the military; the failure of the justice system to protect human rights and to prosecute the perpetrators of such abuses; and government and military responsibility for those abuses.

While acknowledging that human rights abuses exist, members of President Serrano's government deny all responsibility for the violations. They further deny that the military is or should be held accountable for the civil patrols. Members of the government also assert that human rights abuses committed by members of the civil patrols are inevitable in rural Guatemala. They maintain that abolition of civil patrols would violate the constitutional guarantee of freedom of association - that citizens are free to organize community groups.

Military officials deny that human rights violations are committed at all by their own soldiers and they disclaim military involvement in human rights abuses by the civil patrollers and in the persistent attacks against human rights advocates like Amilcar Mendez and CERJ.

Instead, government officials rationalize the existence of 45,000 military troops and more than 500,000 civil patrollers and argue that the anti-government guerilla force of about 800-1500 foot soldiers must be resisted.[1]

The RFK Center condemns the Guatemalan government's denial of responsibility for the pervasive and serious human rights abuses in Guatemala. This report confirms that the civil patrols continue to violate human rights under a protective cloak of impunity. The military uses the civil patrols in the highlands of Guatemala to control the indigenous population and to repress civil and nonviolent dissent. Human rights advocates are systematically targeted and citizens who oppose participation in the civil patrols have been attacked, murdered and accused of being insurgents.

The Guatemalan Government appears to lack the political will to challenge and eradicate human rights abuses. President Serrano has labeled human rights activist Amilcar Mendez a guerilla collaborator. His remarks, and similar allegations from other public officials, denigrate the work of and encourage attacks against human rights advocates like Mendez.

This report focuses attention on human rights violations committed by the

---

[1] *Estimates were obtained in a delegation interview with Captain Yon Rivera in Santa Cruz del Quiche on June 14, 1992.*

members of the civil patrols, the military and the Guatemalan Government since the inauguration of President Serrano in January 1991. Most of the cases of human rights violations detailed in this report were recorded by the author during the past two years while working with CERJ in Guatemala. For the personal protection of witnesses, their names are not used, except when specific permission has been granted to do so, or when the case is already known to the public.

The report is organized in eight sections. Chapter II provides a historical background to human rights in Guatemala and discusses the ongoing repression of the indigenous communities, and the human rights obligations of the Guatemalan Government. Chapter III describes the origin of the civil patrols: their purpose, duties, and relationship with the military. Chapter IV documents human rights violations committed by members of the civil patrols since President Serrano's government came into power. Chapter V examines the Guatemalan military's accountability for the civil patrollers and their conduct. Chapter VI describes the civil government's failure to protect human rights and to bring the civil patrollers, extrajudicial groups, and the military to justice for their illegal actions against human rights advocates, members and leaders of CERJ. This chapter also describes the Government's lack of political will to administer justice and the inadequacy of the judicial system. Chapter VII summarizes the conclusions of this report and Chapter VIII, the final chapter, presents the RFK Center's recommendations to the Government of Guatemala, the U.S. Government and the international community.

The RFK Center calls on everyone concerned about human rights and the people of Guatemala to condemn the Guatemalan government's human rights violations and to take active steps to improve the human rights situation in Guatemala.

II. INTRODUCTION

(1). OVERVIEW.

"The main feature of Guatemalan society today is still the state of fear in which everybody lives."[2]

In the highlands of Guatemala, the military maintains control over the indigenous Mayan population[3] through violence, intimidation and fear. During the last fifteen years, repression has intensified and military domination has been institutionalized through the creation and patronage of "civil defense patrols." During 1982-83, the military regime of General Efrain Rios Montt created these armed civilian units as part of a counterinsurgency strategy to eliminate leftist guerilla forces which successive military and civilian governments have been fighting for thirty years. The civil patrols were exclusively established in rural indigenous communities, and serve as a free militia, performing both military and intelligence tasks for the army. Since their establishment, membership in the civil patrols has varied between 500,000 and one million.

In 1985, a civilian government was elected for the first time after eighteen years of successive military regimes. The new Constitution specifically provided for the protection of human rights, including the right of association. Since Guatemalans are entitled *not* to associate, participation in the civil patrols has become voluntary. The practice, however, differs drastically from the law. Today, members of the civil patrols, under the auspices of the military, quell any opposition to civil patrol service. The civil patrols continue to serve as agents of the military and to bolster military control over the indigenous communities in the highlands of Guatemala.

The Council for Ethnic Communities ("CERJ") was founded in July 1988 by Amilcar Mendez Urizar and members of the indigenous communities to protest against forced recruitment into the civil patrols; to support men who oppose joining the civil patrols; to condemn human rights abuses; and to educate the indigenous communities about their constitutional, human and cultural rights. Because its mandate openly challenges military control of the indigenous sectors, leaders and members of CERJ are subjected to violence and persecution. Since its inception, twenty-five CERJ members have been killed or disappeared[4].

CERJ has filed over four hundred complaints for human rights violations perpetrated against nonpatrollers and CERJ members. In most of these cases, the alleged perpetrators are civil patrollers. To date, no one has been convicted

---

[2] *See the report by the U.N. expert on Guatemala, Christian Tomuschat, U.N. Doc. E/CN. 4/1992/5, paragraph 184, January 21, 1992.*

[3] *Government estimates state that the Guatemalan population is 65 percent Indian, but non-governmental groups provide higher numbers.*

[4] *See appendix 8 to this report for a list of the 25 cases.*

for any of the murders. Only one of the cases proceeded to trial. Members of the civil patrols interfere with and obstruct judicial proceedings, threaten judges and witnesses, and further disobey and evade the law. Many of the indigenous communities remain under military jurisdiction while the civil authorities, including the judiciary, are eclipsed by the civil patrol structure, and efforts to protect human rights are neutralized.

The military disclaims all responsibility for the civil patrols and denies that the Guatemalan armed forces intimidate and coerce indigenous men to serve in the civil patrols. Despite attempts by the armed forces to dissociate themselves from the human rights violations committed by the civil patrollers, the military remains accountable. Members of the military openly threaten non-patrollers and CERJ members and they maintain a particularly brutal campaign of vilification against human rights advocate Amilcar Mendez Urizar.[5] The Minister of Defense is legally responsible for the civil patrol in terms of Decreto 19-86 which ratifies the "Voluntary Civil Self Defense Committees" as part of the military reserves.

The Serrano government lacks the political will to change the military's domination over civilians in the highlands of Guatemala. Not only has the government failed to establish and strengthen civil government and authority, but the legislature has similarly failed to challenge and oust military control over the indigenous communities in the highlands. Oscar Villar Anleu, Vice President of the Congressional Commission for Human Rights, commented:

> "You cannot change the situation to utopia from day to night. People are used to the structures of de facto military governments and psychological intimidation."[6]

The Guatemalan Government accepts the impunity of the military and the civil patrols and, as such, supports human rights violations perpetrated by members of the military and the civil patrols.

In August 1992, peace agreements were signed between the Government and the Guatemalan National Revolutionary Unity guerrilla forces ("URNG")[7] which limit the future role of the civil patrols. The office of the Human Rights Ombudsman is mandated to establish whether the civil patrols are voluntary and to investigate cases of crimes allegedly committed by the civil patrollers. The army agreed not

---

[5] *See appendices 1-5 and 9 to this report, including copies of some of the defamatory pamphlets distributed around Santa Cruz del Quiche. See page 45 (b).*

[6] *Interview by the author with Oscar Villar Anleu on August 26, 1992.*

[7] *The Unidad Revolucionaria Nacional Guatemalteca ("the Guatemalan National Revolutionary Unity") consists of the united guerrilla platform of the four insurgent groups: Fuerzas Armadas Rebeldes ("Armed Rebel Forces, FAR"); Ejercito Guerillero de los Pobres ("Guatemalan Army of the Poor, EGP"); Organizacion Revolucionaria del Pueblo ("Revolutionary Organization of the People, ORPA"); and Partido Guatemalteco de Trabajo ("Guatemalan Workers Party, PGT").*

to encourage an increase of the civil patrols or rearm existing patrols "except when deemed necessary." It was decided that, in such cases, the municipal mayor will call a public meeting and invite the local human rights ombudsman to verify the willingness of the community to perform civil patrol service or to receive more weapons.

The peace accords, however, offer little promise of reversing the entrenched militarization of Guatemala, given the history of military impunity and trespass of the law. In addition, proper implementation of the peace accords and the obligations of the office of the Human Rights Ombudsman cannot be assured.

When he came to power in 1986, President Cerezo intended to verify the voluntary nature of the civil patrol system. Americas Watch expressed concern that such policy could not achieve results:

> "Cerezo rather than abolish the system outright, has stated that representatives of the new government will visit each village and ask residents whether they wish to continue with the civil patrols. He has suggested that this will make patrols voluntary. In theory, the patrols have always been voluntary. In fact, the intimidation inherent in the civil patrol system gives peasants no freedom to oppose the existence of a local civil patrol. A quick visit from a Guatemala City official, however well-intentioned, is unlikely to alter the balance of fear in an isolated community, where the central government traditionally means little compared to local military power."[8]

Eight years later, local and international human rights groups share this apprehension about the peace agreements. Effective verification about the voluntary nature of the civil patrols cannot take place in communities which live in a state of fear and intimidation from the civil patrols. Non-patrollers and human rights activists continue to risk persecution for giving evidence about forced recruitment into the civil patrols.

Prior investigations of abuses of human rights by civil patrollers by representatives from the office of the Human Rights Ombudsman have been limited by threats and attacks from the civil patrollers. Civil patrollers have also interfered with cases which have been pursued. The peace accords do not extend or strengthen the mandate of the Ombudsman's office and offer no new protection against intimidation and impunity. Precedent demonstrates that the government cannot guarantee protection for the Ombudsman's office or for the judiciary to observe the provisions of the peace agreements.

A further obstacle lies in the imprecise language of the peace accords. The military may continue to increase the numbers of civil patrols and rearm them by relying on the qualifying clause "except where it is considered necessary." The military today claims that communities solicit arms for their civil patrols

---

[8] *See the Americas Watch report of August 1986, "Civil Patrols in Guatemala," page 10.*

to protect themselves from attacks by the insurgents. The army employs the same argument to rationalize an increase of the number of civil patrols and of the weapons provided to them. Two days after the peace accords were signed, the head of the Army's press office, Captain Yon Rivera, stated:

> "The government has promised not to promote the creation of more patrollers, but that is provided that conditions are not produced that make them necessary; if the civilian population continues being harassed by the insurgents and solicit to organize themselves, as is their constitutional right, the agreements have as a fundamental condition that the civil populations are not harassed."[9]

Statements such as these increase concern about the military's commitment to uphold the peace accords and to decrease the number of civil patrollers. It remains questionable whether the peace accords will succeed in the existing climate of impunity and fear which dominates rural Guatemala.

(2). HISTORY OF GUATEMALA.

The most populous country in Central America, Guatemala has been described as two countries:[10] a land of the Mayans who mostly live in the rural highlands of Guatemala and who make up 65 percent of Guatemala's nine million inhabitants, and a country of Ladinos, or persons of mixed race.

Since Pedro de Alvarado conquered Guatemala in 1524, the indigenous people have struggled to reclaim their land from the Ladino elite and from multinational corporations. Landowners repressed the indigenous communities to ensure a monopoly of the productive lands and to guarantee cheap labor. Today, Guatemala has the most unequal ownership of land in Latin America: 2 percent of the landowners control 65 percent of the land, while 27 percent of Guatemalans are landless.[11]

Vast differences in economic conditions reflect the disparity of land holdings: 55 percent of Guatemala's gross national product is secured by only 5 percent of the population, whereas 70 percent of the population is unable to meet subsistence levels.[12]

After Haiti and Bolivia, Guatemala has the lowest 'physical quality of life'

---

[9] *See the report in Siglo Veintiuno, "Yon Rivera: Ejercito obedece, respeta y espalda el acuerdo," on August 9, 1992.*

[10] *See the report "Maximizing Deniability: The Justice System and Human Rights in Guatemala," by The International Human Rights Law Group, July 1986, page 40.*

[11] *See Guatemala: A Country Guide [Alberquerque: The Inter American Hemispheric Resource Center, 1989] by Tom Barry.*

[12] *See the Commision Economica para America Latina (CEPAL), as quoted in "The Battle for Guatemala," by Susanne Jonas, published in New York by Westview Press, page 177.*

inthe hemisphere. The majority (67 percent) of Guatemalans live in extreme poverty, 45 percent are illiterate and 66 percent lack access to health care. Every year, 42,000 children die of curable or preventable diseases. The life expectancy of the rural indigenous population is sixteen years shorter than the life expectancy of Ladinos.

Although Guatemala gained independence from Spanish rule in 1821, subsequent governments have not represented the interests of the indigenous population. Real social reform was initiated only during the "ten years of spring" (1945-1954) under Presidents Juan Jose Arevalo and Jacobo Arbenz Guzman. This brief interlude of broad-minded social reform ended when radical land distribution precipitated a coup by the "Liberation Forces" sponsored by the CIA.

In 1962, an armed opposition emerged in response to oppression by the previous regimes. Nationalist-minded military officers joined with the Communist Party to form the Rebel Armed Forces ("FAR"). During the 1970's, two new guerrilla groups were established: the Organization of People in Arms ("ORPA") and the Guerrilla Army of the Poor ("EGP"). In 1982, these guerrilla forces joined with the Guatemalan Workers Party ("PGT") to form the Guatemalan National Revolutionary Unity ("URNG") which now functions as the political and military command of the rebel movement in Guatemala.

Since the advent of the insurgency, Guatemala has been governed primarily through a counter-insurgency policy. During 1966-1968, under the elected President Julio Mendez Montenegro, death squads attacked progressive leaders in Guatemala City. In rural areas almost 8,000 people were killed[13] in attempts to annihilate guerrilla forces and their supporters. These massacres continued during 1970-1973 when about 15,000 people were assassinated under the administration of Colonel Arana.

The insurgency expanded during the late 1970's with 6,000 to 8,000 combatants and almost half a million active supporters.[14] At the same time, popular movements, religious groups and indigenous community activism developed. The military regime of General Romeo Lucas Garcia (1978-1982) reacted to the growing opposition with the cruelest show of violence in modern Guatemalan history. From 1978-1984, 100,000 people were killed and 40,000 people disappeared. Hundreds of villages were destroyed and 750,000 Guatemalans were internally displaced. Over 250,000 refugees fled Guatemala and this reign of terror. The majority of these victims were non-combatants, but the regime justified the murderous crackdown as essential to the eradication of a violent communist uprising.

In 1982, General Efrain Rios Montt staged a successful coup. General Montt's year-long rule was renowned for its efforts to eliminate corruption in urban Guatemala and for its consolidation of military control in the rural

---

[13] See "The Battle for Guatemala," by Susanne Jonas, supra, page 63.
[14] See "The Battle for Guatemala," supra, page 138.

areas. General Montt dismissed the Guatemalan Congress and suspended the Constitution. His new counterinsurgency program, the National Security and Development Plan ("PSND"), shifted from brutal violence to a campaign of rural pacification. Indigenous people were contained in military controlled areas called "model villages" or "development poles." The civil patrols were simultaneously created as part of this counterinsurgency strategy. The command structures of General Montt's strategy (called "Victory 82") persist to this day through the civil patrols and the militarization of the highland communities.

In August 1983, Minister of Defense, General Oscar Humberto Mejia Victores deposed General Montt as head of state. An elected constituent assembly drafted a new Constitution and, on January 1, 1986, Vinicio Cerezo Arevalo was inaugurated as the first civilian president of Guatemala in twenty years.

During the first two years of President Cerezo's government, human rights abuses declined, nongovernmental human rights groups were established, popular community groups reemerged in rural Guatemala, and unions were reorganized in the cities. However, expectations that Cerezo could curb the political violence were shortlived. Military intolerance of the growing grassroots organizations soon led to a crackdown on these indigenous and human rights groups. Security forces continued to assassinate, disappear, and harass human rights activists. President Cerezo refused to investigate and his tenuous rule was further weakened by two unsuccessful coup attempts in May 1988 and May 1989. Near the end of Cerezo's administration, human rights violations soared.

When Jorge Serrano Elias, the presidential candidate from the rightwing Movement of Solidarity Action ("MAS"), took office in January 1991, the transfer of power from one civilian government to another was lauded abroad and in Guatemala. Hopes of change increased with President Serrano's promise of a "total peace plan" to end the civil war, to improve the appalling human rights record, and to punish criminals without exception. In August 1991, Serrano announced the formation of a cabinet level Human Rights Commission ("COPREDEH") to respond to human rights violations and to advise the President.

Those early, promising signs were soon to fail. Peace talks are stalled on the subject of human rights, and although the military's impunity has been challenged on occasion, the overall human rights situation has deteriorated since 1991, with Guatemala again descending into a spiral of fear and violence.

The office of the Human Rights Ombudsman recorded 456 extra-judicial executions in 1991, and by June 1992 had received 253 complaints of extra-judicial killings. The Archbishop's office for Human Rights documented 575 extra-judicial executions in 1991. The Guatemalan Human Rights Commission reported more than 400 extra-judicial executions and 50 disappearances by August 1992. Torture, attacks and illegal detentions continue under the Serrano administration. Prominent political and religious figures have been assassinated. The press and political activists have been terrorized by death threats and suffered bomb attacks. Human rights activists who challenge this violence and appeal for respect of the rule of law are routinely attacked. The U.S. Department of State reports that:

> "In 1991, the military, civil patrols, and police continued to commit a majority of the human rights abuses, including extrajudicial killings, torture, and disappearances of, among others, human rights activists, unionists, indigenous people, and street children."[15]

Today, 46,000 refugees remain in exile in Mexico and a million citizens are internally displaced, fearful of returning home to their communities.

(3). HUMAN RIGHTS OBLIGATIONS OF THE GUATEMALAN GOVERNMENT.

Guatemala's Constitution and the international covenants on human and political rights to which Guatemala is a signatory provide an adequate legal framework for the protection of the life and liberty to Guatemalans.

The Constitution ("Constitucion Politica de La Republica de Guatemala," adopted in January 1986) provides a legal basis for the protection of human rights and recognizes the supremacy of international law over the Constitution and other national laws. The Constitution incorporates obligations in terms of international treaties and covenants into domestic law. The Guatemalan Congress approved the United Nations Covenant on Civil and Political Rights ("UNCCPR") on February 19, 1992. Guatemala is also signatory to the American Convention on Human Rights ("ACHR")[16] and to the U.N. Charter and Declaration of Human Rights ("UNCDHR").[17] Both the American Convention on Human Rights and the United Nations Covenant on Civil and Political Rights contain clauses which impose affirmative obligations on signatory parties to ensure that citizens may enjoy these rights and provide remedies to those citizens whose rights have been violated.

Guatemala is also party to International Labor Conventions, which prohibit "all work or service which is exacted from any person under the menace of any

---

[15] *See U.S. Department of State Country Reports on Human Rights Practices for 1991, Report Submitted to The Committee on Foreign Affairs House of Representatives and the Committee on Foreign Relations U.S. Senate by the Department of State ("USDOS 1991 Report").*

[16] *The date of Deposit for Ratification was May 25, 1978.*

[17] *While the Universal Declaration of Human Rights has been considered as a guiding principle rather than a binding law, Article 8 of the Guatemalan Human Rights Law establishes the Declaration as a source of law. See Roberto Lemus Garza for the Procurador de los Derechos Humanos in "Convenciones, Tratados, Pactos y Otros Instrumentos Sobre Derechos Humanos de los cuales La Republica de Guatemala es Parte," Publication No. 3-90 (Guatemala, 1990).*

penalty and for which the said person has not offered himself voluntarily." Also prohibited is forced labor as a means of political coercion, a method of mobilizing labor for economic development, and of racial or social discrimination. Signatory countries are obliged to take effective measures to secure the immediate and complete abolition of forced or compulsory labor as specified by the convention.

Guarantees of political, civil and individual rights and liberties are protected in the Constitution of the Republic of Guatemala. The Government is responsible for insuring the life, liberty, justice, security, peace and personal integrity of its inhabitants (Article 2). The Constitution also provides for the right to security of the person (Article 1); the right to life (Article 3); the right to engage in lawful activities (Article 5); the right of peaceful assembly and public demonstration (Article 33); the right of freedom of association, including the right *not* to associate (Article 34); the right of freedom of expression (Article 35); the right to take action against infringements of human rights, including the right to lodge public complaints against violators of such rights and to seek prosecution for punishment of guilty parties (Article 45); the right to freedom of movement (Article 25); and the prohibition of the registration of persons unless it is done by uniformed security forces with "just cause for it" (Article 26).

The Constitution also provides legal protection for detainees. No one may be detained without a warrant of arrest (Article 6). The detainee may not to be taken to any secret detention center (Article 10) and must appear before a competent judicial authority within six hours after his or her arrest (Article 6). The detainee must immediately be informed of the reasons for the detention (Article 6 and 7) and has the right to be interrogated only by judicial authorities. Extrajudicial testimony is inadmissible (Article 9). The Constitution forbids the practice of secret or special tribunals and other proceedings which are not lawfully established (Article 12).

The indigenous population enjoys special protection under the Constitution for their customs, forms of social organization, culture and the provision and protection of land. (Articles 66-70).

Article 263 of the Guatemalan Constitution provides for the substantial remedy of *habeas corpus* which is directed specifically at illegal detentions, but which also provides the opportunity for judicial relief in cases of death threats. The *habeas corpus* remedy provides that an individual unlawfully detained or oppressed shall immediately be "liberated, guaranteed freedom, or released from the degradation or coercion that he or she has gone through."[18] The remedy requires that the detainee must be brought before a judge within twenty-four hours after his detention; that the official responsible for the illegal detention is subject to criminal prosecution; that the police help to find

---

[18] See "Crisis Point, Human Rights in Guatemala under President Serrano," by the Center for Human Rights and Constitutional Law ("the Center") and the Guatemala Support Network, published in October, 1992 by the Center, page 93.

the detainee and inform the courts of any relevant evidence; and that the judge visits the place of detention to assure the release of the detainee.

Ongoing human rights violations in Guatemala clearly do not observe these Constitutional and international standards. The promise of civilian and democratic rule has yet to be fulfilled, and the peace process recently initiated between the Serrano administration and the insurgent URNG has little chance of success in the existing milieu of impunity and fear.

III. CIVIL PATROLS WERE CREATED TO "CONTROL" THE PEOPLE

(1). THE MILITARY CREATED THE CIVIL PATROLS.[19]

The Guatemalan government initiated a new counterinsurgency campaign during 1982-1984 (called "Victory '82") in the Guatemalan highlands to eradicate the guerilla movement. Central to this campaign was the creation of civil patrols. The civil patrols were established in rural communities which overwhelmingly consisted of indigenous people. Although the civil patrols formally consisted of "conscripts" of men between eighteen and sixty years, many boys as young as twelve, and men as old as seventy, were forced to serve.

With the establishment of the civil patrols, the military achieved a permanent and institutionalized militarization of the highlands of Guatemala. Indeed, one of the four objectives of the military's invention of the civil patrols was to "control...the people."[20] The civil patrollers provided the military with free day-and-night surveillance in rural communities; informants about all local activities; cannon fodder for combat; and a means to control any local opposition, without a formal military presence in these communities.

(2). INDIGENOUS MEN WERE FORCED TO PATROL.

The army called community meetings all over the highlands and ordered the local men to do civil patrol duty. Objections were met with punishment. Those who objected were labelled subversives, which often meant that they would be killed.

This testimony from Chichicastenango, Quiche illustrates how the civil patrols were established by force:

> "My village was destroyed by the military in 1982 and we all had to leave the area for some time. After we returned, the Commander of the army base came and said that we had to form a civil patrol to control all the activities in the town. He had a document prepared and everyone had to sign it to verify their commitment to the civil patrols. The commander advised that if people refused to sign it, it would be taken as proof that they were guerrillas and something would happen to them. Therefore everyone signed it. He then said if people refused to do service they would be called subversives, and killed."[21]

---

[19] *For a thorough early history of civil patrols, see the report by Americas Watch, "Civil Patrols in Guatemala," published in August, 1986.*

[20] *This was taken from "Annex H: Standing Orders for the Development of Counterinsurgency Operations," an army document published in July 1982. See America's watch report, "Civil Patrols in Guatemala," of 1986, page 20 for discussion of Annex H.*

[21] *This testimony and all the following testimonies in this chapter were taken by the author and a representative from the Center for Human Rights Legal Action ("CHRLA") in interviews with witnesses in Santa Cruz del Quiche, during July 1992.*

(3). MEN WHO DID NOT PATROL WERE PUNISHED.

Once the civil patrol was established in the communities, patrol commanders were left in charge of enforcing duties and participation in the patrols. The army instructed the commanders to punish those who refused duty, failing which they would be punished themselves.

Four peasants from different communities of the Quiche region described the penalties and fines which were enforced for refusing to patrol or for missing patrol duty, as follows.

A former civil patroller from Chiul, a village in northern Quiche, reported retribution against four men in 1984 when they refused to patrol:

> "The four men were accused of being guerrillas by the civil patrollers. Officers from the local military garrison summoned the civil patrol commander for a meeting. When he returned, he ordered the civil patrol members to get the men from their homes, detain them, and take them to the military garrison. The patrollers carried out their orders and the four men were never seen again."

A witness from Chichicastenango said:

> "If a person couldn't patrol, he had to pay ten quetzales. For example, if he went to the coast to work, or to the city, he had to pay this fine. If he couldn't pay, the patrol chiefs had to inform the army detachment and then he would be put into a well which was fifteen meters deep, containing one meter of water. This well was built by the community under the orders of the military detachment to be used as a punishment for those who refused to patrol, or couldn't patrol."

A witness from Joyobaj described his experiences:

> "If a person didn't patrol he had to do unpaid road work for three days. The civil patrol leaders were told by the army lieutenant to enforce that."

Another witness from Joyobaj stated that:

> "On several occasions if men did not want to serve, the patrol leader would tie them to a tree. Also, if their wives protested, they, too, would be tied to trees."

(4). THE MILITARY TRAINED CIVIL PATROLLERS TO CONTROL THEIR COMMUNITIES AND ELIMINATE THE OPPOSITION.

Patrollers typically were ordered by the army to police the streets of their village day and night; to control the comings and goings of the village inhabitants; to stop and interrogate any strangers entering the town; and to report suspicious behavior by neighbors to the local army base commander.

Military "commissioners" (ex soldiers, armed and paid by the military to act on their behalf within the communities) assisted with these surveillance and control duties. The commissioners were often secretly appointed by the military and were responsible for intelligence reports and conscription into the army.

In Quiche, all inhabitants were required to carry a pass, signed by their civil patrol commander, stating where they were going, and granting them military permission to travel.[22] A witness from Joyobaj, Quiche reported that the civil patrol commanders forced peasants who left to work on the coastal plantations to report to the local military detachment and to produce their passes as proof that they were going to work.

Civil patrollers were instructed by the military to eliminate the opposition, including anyone suspected of criticizing the civil patrol system. Elimination involved capturing suspected dissenters and turning them over to the military, where they were often tortured, beaten, and sometimes killed. A civil patroller from Zacualpa, Quiche describes some of the methods of "elimination" used by the army:

> "In 1983, the army arrived in my village and called a meeting of all the men. They said that they had a list of "bad people" who refused to patrol, and the army official read out their names. These men were then captured by the army, and taken to the military detachment in Zacualpa. Two days later they were released. They told the community that they had been interrogated by military officers about guerilla activity in the area. When they replied that they didn't know anything, they were given electric shock torture by soldiers. They said that the torturers burnt their mouths with "sticks of fire". Two days after their return, soldiers came and recaptured them. Their bodies were never discovered."

Another peasant from Chichicastenango stated that the civil patrol commanders in his village were required to perform these tasks themselves:

> "On February 20, 1984, the civil patrollers called a meeting. All the people in the town were there. The leaders of the civil patrol said that they had received a note from the army with a list of names of subversives who were to be detained and delivered to the army base. Half the patrollers were worried and didn't want to cooperate, but they realized that they had to. My name appeared on the list of three. First we had our hands and arms tied by the civil patrol commanders and they put us in the town well. At 10:00 p.m. the civil patrol commanders returned from the military detachment and took us out of the well, saying that the army had said that we were bad people and that we were going to be buried in the nearest clearing. The patrollers then killed the two other men with knives and machetes in front of me. I managed to loosen the ropes and ran away and was able to escape."

---

[22] *Two copies of such passes are enclosed as appendices 6 and 7 to this report.*

(5). CIVIL PATROLLERS OPERATE IN COMBAT.

An Americas Watch report confirmed in 1986 that civil patrollers were compelled to search mountainous areas in search of guerrillas:

> "The men must be available for *rastreos* [army-accompanied sweeps.] These *rastreos* can last anywhere from one day to several weeks [during which] the patrollers are often forced to carry out the terrible task of eliminating anyone they find."

Civil patrollers would go into combat in military operations and were deployed in the front lines of battle as "cannon fodder:"

> "The civil patrol must walk in the vanguard, with rank and file troops in the middle and the commander bringing up the rear, thus exposing the patrol unit to the first wave of possible assault even though the patrollers are often unarmed."

(6). THE MILITARY EXTORTED FREE LABOR FROM CIVIL PATROLLERS.

Americas Watch quoted the current Archbishop of Guatemala as follows about how civilians were used by the military as free labor in the department of San Marcos:

> "Men were forced to work on roads so that the army could pass through more easily."[23]

A witness from the Chichicastenango area further reported that each patroller was required to take two loads of firewood a year to the military garrison in Chichicastenango.

(7). THE MILITARY SUPERVISED CIVIL PATROL ACTIVITIES.

High command army officials claimed that the civil patrols were independently and spontaneously organized, but General Guillermo Echeverria Vielman wrote in 1983 to President Rios Montt that:

> "The civilian defense patrols are led, controlled, protected, and work under the military's vigilance; thus they are part of the army."[24]

In fact, military supervision was tight. Patrol leaders visited the local army base every eight days in some areas and every two weeks in other places to report on activities in their communities and to receive instructions from the

---

[23] *See the Americas Watch report "Civil Patrols in Guatemala," supra, page 57.*
[24] *See the open letter from General Guillermo Echeverria Vielman to President Efrain Rios Montt, on January 11, 1983. See Americas Watch report "Civil Patrols in Guatemala," supra, page 41.*

military commander about present military strategy. Civil patrollers from Joyobaj and Zacualpa described their obligations as civil patrol commanders as follows:

> "I was the civil patrol leader from 1982-1988. I had to report to the base every week. The commander would ask me if people were performing their service and if I had punished those who didn't. They would tell me that service was obligatory and those that did not do it were guerrillas, and that I must enforce civil patrol duty."

The other civil patrol commander stated that:

> "I was the chief of the civil patrol for six years until 1988. Every Thursday and Sunday the chiefs were made to report to the base to receive orientation. Every Thursday the chiefs would call the people in the community to a meeting and would tell them what the army had told us to say: that they all had to continue patrolling, that everyone had to control their neighbor so as to avoid wallowing in subversion, and that those that didn't patrol were bad people."

(8). CONCLUSIONS.

The military created the civil patrols to serve as instruments in its counter-insurgency strategy and to consolidate military domination of rural communities. The civil patrols were established "to augment the army's military strength and intelligence in areas of conflict, and, more importantly, to provide vigilance and control of the local population, preventing any form of independent political organization."[25]

---

[25] See the Americas Watch report, "Civil Patrols in Guatemala," supra, page 2.

IV. CIVIL PATROLS VIOLATE HUMAN RIGHTS

(1). CIVIL PATROLS MAINTAIN POWER OVER THE INDIGENOUS PEOPLE.

Civil patrollers have continued to perform the same military duties and violate the human rights of their fellow citizens under the Serrano administration. The U.N. expert on Guatemala, Christian Tomuschat, concludes that:

> "[The civil patrols] have become an institutionalized element of uncontrollable violence."[26]

Although civil patrol duty is voluntary under the 1985 Constitution,[27] Tomuschat reports that:

> "Contrary to what is indicated, many inhabitants of the rural areas continue to be compelled to join the ranks of patrols. Anyone who refuses to join a patrol is accused of being a guerrilla or of collaborating with the guerillas and is persecuted, threatened, ill treated or tortured or even extrajudicially executed."[28]

Furthermore civil patrollers attack and harrass members of human rights organizations who challenge the power of the military establishment. CERJ leaders and members are specifically targeted and harassed by civil patrollers and the military because they expose human rights abuses perpetrated by the patrollers.

In many highland communities in Guatemala the civil patrols continue to exert "control" over the residents. A civil patroller from San Pedro Jocopilas describes how the civil patrols function in his village and describes some of the human rights abuses committed by the civil patrollers:

> "I only do my service because I am afraid of being killed like the others who have quit. In patrol meetings the civil patrol leaders say that it is obligatory, and that there are articles in the constitution that say so. We know that is not true but we are scared for our lives. In a meeting in May, one patroller protested that he knew that the patrols were voluntary under Article 34 [of the Constitution], and that the service was pointless because we did not have enough arms to protect ourselves if the guerrillas did come. The commanders got very angry and said that he must be a guerilla. They say that those that do not patrol are working against the people. We patrol every two weeks for twenty-four

---

[26] *See report by Christian Tomuschat, U.N. Doc. E/CN.41199215, January 21, 1992, paragraph 193.*

[27] *Article 34 of the Constitution provides that "no one is obliged to be associated with, or form a part of, self-defense committees."*

[28] *See Christian Tomuschat's report, supra, paragraph 193.*

hours. There are boys as young as twelve doing their turns. If someone does not turn up for their turn, the chiefs threaten that they will have to work for the municipality for eight days without pay. We also have to pay fines of six to ten quetzales each time we miss a turn. The civil patrol leaders meet with the army and the municipal patrol commander every eight days to be oriented, and then they meet with us and tell us that the army says that we must patrol or there will be consequences."[29]

(a). The civil patrollers force indigenous men to participate in the patrols.

Personal safety in rural Guatemala depends on conforming to military structures and participating in the civil patrols. Some civil patrol leaders have gained powerful positions in the community through their military connections and they pursue military policies with vigor. Many patrollers, however, participate under duress.[30]

Those who challenge the civil patrol structure are labelled "communists" or "subversives" by military officials, soldiers and civil patrol commanders. In the context of the Guatemalan government's civil war against leftist insurgents, being labelled a subversive often precedes violence against the accused and serves as a rationalization for human rights abuses.

(b). Non-patrollers are assassinated.

Since the civil patrols were created, widespread persecution has followed men who resist participation in the patrols. The U.S. State Department reports that:

> "Credible reports say that those who refuse to serve in the civil patrols have suffered serious abuse, including death."[31]

The following cases describe the assassination of men who refused to participate in the civil patrols:

> On March 15, 1991, Pablo Ajiataz Chivalan and Manuel Ajiataz Chivalan were assassinated in Santabal I, a community of San Pedro Jocopilas. There is strong reason to believe that civil patrollers killed them. According to eyewitness accounts, the two brothers were ha-

---

[29] *Interview by the author with civil patrol member from San Pedro Jocopilas on July 4, 1992.*

[30] *Testimonies taken by the author about forced recruitment were received from victims in the provinces of Totonicapon, Quiche, and Solola. For further testimony about continued forced recruitment into the civil patrols in Huehuetenango, see "Civiles entre tres fuegos," a 1991 report by the Guatemalan Archbishop's Office for Human Rights.*

[31] *See USDOS 1991 Report, section 1, f.*

rassed by the civil patrol commander and accused of being guerrillas because they did not do their service.[32]

Miguel Barrera Calel was assassinated in Santabal I, San Pedro Jocopilas on April 19, 1991. In a complaint filed on April 30, 1991 with the office of the Government Ombudsman for Human Rights in Quiche, Marcelina Calel (Calel's mother) confirms that he had received numerous death threats from the civil patrol chief of their community for not participating in the civil patrols.[33]

Camilo Ajqui Jimon was stabbed to death by three men in front of his house in Portrero Viejo, Zacualpa, Quiche on April 14, 1991. Witnesses state that he had received a series of death threats from civil patrol chiefs for not participating in the patrols.[34]

Miguel Tiu Imul was shot to death at 7:30 pm on November 30th, 1991. His assassination took place thirty meters from his house in Canton de los Montanas, Parraxtut, Sacapulas. Military commissioners and civil patrol chiefs Domingo Castro Lux, Pedro Ixcotoyac, Juan Lux Castro and Juan de Leon Perez are accused of committing the murder because of previous threats by these men against Miguel Tiu Imul and other members of the community. In July 1991, Tiu Imul stopped patrolling because he was sixty-five years old. He had been captured in July 1987 by civil patrol chiefs and military commissioners and taken to the military base in Chiul where he was tortured and interrogated by soldiers and officers for three days. Two days later, fifty soldiers had arrived at his house and severely beat him. The civil patrols and military commissioners kept a close watch on his house after the assault on Tiu Imul.[35]

Catarino Chanchavac Larios was beheaded on August 26, 1992 in San Pablo, San Pedro Jocopilas. Witnesses report that he had received death threats from the civil patrol chief of the neighboring village Santabal II days before his death, for refusing to patrol.[36]

(c). Civil patrollers threaten and intimidate non-patrollers.

The CERJ office in Santa Cruz del Quiche daily receives reports about

---

[32] *Interview by author with witnesses from Santabal I, in Santa Cruz del Quiche on July 4, 1992.*
[33] *Interview by author with Marcelina Calel, Santa Cruz del Quiche, July 7, 1992.*
[34] *Interview by CHRLA representative with men from Portrero Viejo, in Santa Crvz del Quiche, July 21, 1992.*
[35] *Interview by the author with Tiu Imul's wife and daughter and citizens from Parraxtut during December 1991.*
[36] *Testimony by witnesses to CERJ on August 31, 1992.*

intimidation by civil patrollers against non-patrollers. Men who quit the patrols are threatened in attempts to coerce them to return to patrol duty and to frighten patrol members into submission, as illustrated by the following cases:

> In May and June 1992, leaflets of guerrilla propaganda were distributed around San Pedro Jocopilas. Civil patrol commanders accused the non-patrollers of being responsible for the propaganda. In July 1992, guerillas attacked the area. Civil patrol chiefs again blamed the non-patrollers for the attack.[37]

Such accusations imply that non-patrollers are acting outside the law simply because they have terminated their patrol service. As previously stated, in Guatemala such accusations are synonymous with death threats.

> Witnesses report that in June 1992, civil patrol commanders in San Pedro Jocopilas publicly called for a change to a military government to enable them to "eliminate" [assassinate] non-patrollers.[38]

> On April 21, 1992, a former civil patrol commander from Cruzche, Quiche was told by the existing patrol commander that he would soon be killed, because he was not collaborating with them anymore.[39]

> On January 21, 1992, after several years of harassment, seven villages from the municipality of Joyobaj filed a complaint with the office of the local government Ombudsman for Human Rights protesting that they were forced to perform patrol duty and constantly received death threats from patrol chiefs and military commissioners as a result of their resignation from the civil patrols.[40]

> On May 17, 1992, a former soldier and civil patroller, Jose Cux de La Cruz, entered the house of Maria Garcia in Tunaja, Quiche and told her that the military commissioner, Mariano Morente Lopez, had sent him to capture her son, a non-patroller, because he was a guerrilla. He wielded a machete and threatened Maria Garcia with death if she did not give up her son.[41]

(d). Civil patrollers shoot and beat non-patrollers.

Civil patrollers not only verbally threaten but also physically attack non-patrollers:

---

[37] *Interview by the author with a witness from San Pedro Jocopilas in July 1992 and testimony to CERJ on April 12, 1992.*
[38] *Testimony to CERJ on June 14, 1992.*
[39] *Testimony to CERJ on April 25, 1992.*
[40] *Complaint filed with the office of the Human Rights Ombudsman in Santa Cruz del Quiche on January 21, 1992.*
[41] *See complaint filed to the justice of the peace, Santa Cruz del Quiche, May 19, 1992.*

Civil patrollers shot at a non-patroller, Tomas Capir Set, on January 12, 1992 as he approached his house in Chunima, Chichicastenango. Fortunately, Capir survived because he was not struck by the bullets.[42]

On May 25, 1992, Manuel Chingo Gomez, a civil patroller and military commissioner, accused a non-patroller, Terrazzo Grave Hernandez, in Tunaja, Zacualpa of collaborating with the guerillas. He then kicked and beat Terrazzo. When Terrazzo escaped, Manuel Chingo threatened him, shouting: "Your life is in danger. We have your name in the military zone. You will not escape death." Terrazzo was one of the leaders who called for an end to the civil patrol in Tunaja.[43]

Men from the municipality of San Pedro Jocopilas reported that civil patrol members on night duty frequently fire bullets into the air near houses of the non-patrollers to scare them into patrol duty.[44]

(e). Civil patrollers discriminate against non-patrollers in community projects.

Some civil patrollers exclude non-patrollers from participation in local community projects. A man from a village in Santa Cruz del Quiche reported that civil patrol members prohibited his children from entering the school, because he was not participating in the civil patrols, and that they threatened that he would be excluded from community projects such as receiving potable water or electricity.[45] In a nearby community the civil patrollers cut off water services to the houses of non-patrollers. The commander asserted that he had the Governor's authority to cut off water to those who do not patrol.[46]

(f). Minors are forced to patrol.

Forced recruitment of minors into the civil patrols is widespread in the highlands of Guatemala.[47] During 1992, boys as young as ten were forced to perform twenty-four-hour unpaid patrol service every week.[48]

A witness from Joyobaj said that his patrol duty started in 1982, when he

---

[42] *Testimony to the author in January 1992. See the Chunima case, Chapter VI, section 4 (f).*
[43] *Interview by the RFK delegation with members of the Tunaja community on June 14, 1992 in Santa Cruz del Quiche.*
[44] *Interview by the author with members of the community San Pedro Jocopilas in July 1992.*
[45] *CERJ records of a complaint filed on January 2, 1992.*
[46] *Testimony to CERJ on June 6, 1992.*
[47] *Interviews by the author with witnesses from Solala, Totonicapan, and Quiche in 1992.*
[48] *Interview by the author with a young witness from Chichicastenango on July 15, 1992.*

was twelve years old. He was armed and sent on a military sweep within the first weeks of his duty. He once missed his patrol duty and was put in a well for twelve hours as punishment.[49]

Children's rights are protected from such exploitation and violence under the United Nations Conventions on the Rights of the Child and codified under Guatemalan legislation.

(g). Sanctions are imposed against patrollers who miss civil patrol duty.

Throughout the highlands of Guatemala, patrollers are punished for missing patrol duty. Today, some civil patrol commanders are extorting the equivalent of the minimum daily wage for every absence of twenty- four hours.[50] The economic consequences of these fines are dire. Indigenous men are subsistence farmers and wage earners and they are rarely paid the legal minimum wage. Fear of these fines further compels men to participate in the civil patrols.

A witness from the Santa Cruz del Quiche municipality reported that he had missed four shifts of civil patrol duty during 1991. His family paid the fines to the local patrol commander, but when the young man returned to the community, the commander denied having received any money and forced him to perform double service as an extra penalty.[51]

(2). THE CIVIL PATROLS ATTACK ORGANIZATIONS LIKE CERJ WHICH OPPOSE THE CIVIL PATROL SYSTEM.

Under President Serrano's administration, CERJ continues to battle for its own survival and for the physical safety of its leaders and members. Since its inception in 1988, violations against CERJ have intensified. Almost half of the twenty-five murders of CERJ members occurred during the Sertano administration. The organization has also recorded over four hundred disappearances, kidnappings, physical attacks, threats and other forms of intimidation of its members. Civil patrollers alleged to have perpetrated these crimes have evaded prosecution.

(a). CERJ members are assassinated.

CERJ members are persecuted and assassinated because of their association with CERJ, as illustrated by the following cases:

> On February 17, 1991, two prominent CERJ activists, Juan Perebal Xirum and his son, Manuel Perebal Morales, were shot and killed on the road from their village Chunima to Chupol, Chichicastenango.

---

[49] *Interview by the author with a CERJ member from Joyobaj.*
[50] *Interviews by the author with patrollers from San Pedro Jocopilas, Chichicastenango, and Cruzche during July 1992.*
[51] *Testimony to CERJ, 1991.*

Another son, Diego, survived the attack, but he remains paralyzed from the waist down. The Perebal family was shot by six men, two of whom were subsequently identified by Diego and two other eye witnesses as civil patrol chiefs from Chunima: Manuel Perebal Ajzalam and Manuel Leon Lares. Each of the three victims were previously threatened by Chunima civil patrollers because of their work with CERJ. Manuel and Diego Perebal were primary eyewitnesses in a legal trial where one of the accused violators, Manuel Perebal Ajzalam, was accused of the disappearance of CERJ leader, Sebastian Velasquez Mejia, on October 6, 1991.[52]

Celestino Culaj Vicente was assassinated on June 29, 1991 in San Pedro Jocopilas when he returned home from a festival. He had previously received several death threats from local civil patrol leaders for leaving the patrol and for being a CERJ member. Celestino's wife, Maria Lolmet Xom, reported that the civil patrol commander in their community of Chutzalic had often accused Celestino of being a guerrilla. The civil patrol leaders in San Pedro Jocopilas convened a meeting before the festival and threatened to kill any CERJ members who attended the festival.[53]

(b). CERJ members are disappeared.

The term "disappearance," used throughout Latin America, originated in Guatemala, and is used to describe the unlawful and forceful abduction of a person who is indefinitely held against his or her will and whose whereabouts remain unknown. It is estimated that more than 40,000 Guatemalans have been "disappeared" since 1960. This cruel form of elimination continues to plague the families of victims with uncertainty and leaves them with a glimmer of hope that the victim may reappear. Since the inception of the Serrano administration, two CERJ members have disappeared:

Santos Toj Reyenoso, an active CERJ member, was kidnapped in Guatemala City on May 26, 1991. His body has never been found. Santos participated in human rights courses and was nominated as the CERJ delegate in Cruzche IV, a community outside Santa Cruz del Quiche. Civil patrollers forced Santos to flee Cruzche IV on May 6, 1991

---

[52] *See the case study of Chunima in Chapter VI, 4 (f) for a more detailed account of the events in Chunima. Also see the Americas Watch report, "Guatemala: Slaying of Rights Activists, Impunity Prevails Under New Government," of April 14, 1991.*

[53] *Interview by the author with Celestino's wife and other civil patrollers from San Pedro Jocopilas in Santa Cruz del Quiche, July 7, 1992.*

after they had threatened him with death because of his CERJ activities.[54]

Esteban Tojin disappeared from Mixco, Guatemala City on March 13, 1992. He was displaced from Cruzche II in the municipality of Santa Cruz del Quiche after severe and consistent threats by military commissioners and civil patrol commanders because of his activities with CERJ. Esteban Tojin performed patrol duty until he fled from Cruzche II for his life. At the end of February 1992, Esteban Tojin was chased down the street in Mixco by six of the military commissioners and patrol chiefs from Cruzche II. They shouted after him "run away now, but we will kill you later." His body has never been found.[55]

(c). CERJ members are threatened.

Civil patrollers routinely threaten, intimidate and harass CERJ members. Civil patrollers control the movements of CERJ members, accuse them of collaborating with the guerrillas, and threaten CERJ members with death. The following two cases serve as illustrations of such threats:

In May 1992, in a village in the municipality Santa Lucia Totonicapan, CERJ members who participated in demonstrations were under strict surveillance by the local civil patrollers and military commissioners. Military commissioners pronounced that "those with Runujel Junam (CERJ) have to be eliminated. We are only waiting for a government order to kill them one by one.[56]"

Miguel Tojin Ixcoy from Cruzche II filed a complaint with the office of the Ombudsman for Human Rights about a civil patrol leader, Martin Tojin Ixcoy, who had threatened Miguel on several occasions. Miguel reported that Martin asked if he was a CERJ member. Martin added: "I hope not, because the people who work with human rights are the roots of the subversion, they are bad weeds, and they need to be plucked out of the community."

(3). THE CIVIL PATROLS WIELD UNCONSTITUTIONAL AUTHORITY IN COMMUNITIES.

The civil patrollers abuse their authority and wield illegal and unconstitutional authority over the rural communities. They usurp police powers, conduct unlawful arrests, and carry out unauthorized, intrusive surveillance. Civil

---

[54] *See CERJ records of May 1991.*
[55] *Interview by the RFK delegation with Maria Tojin Ixcoy, Esteban's mother, and Catarina Lux Zapeta, Esteban's wife, in Santa Cruz del Quiche, June 14, 1992.*
[56] *Testimony to CERJ on May 16, 1992.*

patrol commanders use their power to force patrollers to perform hours of unpaid labor in non-patrol tasks. Miguel Tojin Ixcoy described his experience with Martin Tojin Ixcoy, the civil patrol chief in Cruzche II:

> "He feels superior to everyone only because he has the position of patrol chief. He believes he is the owner of our lives and he can do what he likes. He abuses his power."[57]

(a). Illegal arrests.

Civil patrollers illegally arrest and detain members of the indigenous communities in rural Guatemala. A witness describes the following unlawful detention by civil patrollers in Xeciquel, Cunen, in the province Quiche:

> From May 24 to May 27, 1991, civil patrol commanders and military commissioners Diego Sosa, Santos Rivas Lopez, Santos Pastor Hernandez and Cesario Sosa Us kidnapped six men in Xeciquel, and illegally detained them in the local school until May 28, 1991. During the detention they interrogated and accused the men (Siverio Pastor Itzep, Rolando Pastor Hernandez, Pablo Itzep Hernandez, Siverio Pastor Itzep II, Tiadoro Pastor Itzep, and Francisco Pastor Hernandez) of participating in guerrilla activities.
>
> The civil patrol chiefs and military commissioners took their hostages to the military base in Santa Cruz del Quiche on May 29, 1991. The military commissioners threatened the captives with death if they did not confess that they collaborated with the guerrillas. The next day, the six men were forced by the military commissioners to go to the office of the Ombudsman for Human Rights in Quiche where, under duress, the six men signed a confession admitting their alleged involvement with the guerrillas. The document was prepared before they arrived and was read to them by the Ombudsman before they signed it. The hostages later reported that they had signed the confessions only because they had been threatened with death by the military commissioners and civil patrollers. One of the captives stated after his release that civil patrol chiefs and military commissioners are paid by the military for each guerrilla captured.
>
> On June 6, 1991, one of the victims, Pablo Hernandez Itzep, reported the incident to CERJ. On the same day, Pablo and Amilcar Mendez met with President Serrano to discuss the kidnapping and threats. President Serrano personally guaranteed Pablo's safety during the meeting. Pablo returned to his town the following day. As he descended from the

---

[57] *Author's interview with Miguel Tojin Ixcoy in Santa Cruz del Quiche, June 1992.*

bus, the civil patrol commanders immediately arrested him and threatened him with death for going to a human rights group to report the incident.[58]

(b). Illegal forced labor.

The civil patrols also force members of the indigenous communities to render free labor and to pay "dues" to the civil patrol chiefs. A civil patrol member from San Pedro Jocopilas reported that:

> "In June 1992, the chief of the civil patrol of the municipality of San Pedro Jocopilas, Francisco Ixcoy, forced each civil patrol member to pay five quetzales and the traders to pay fifty quetzales for the annual fiesta. When a patroller said that he could not pay, Francisco accused of him of being a guerrilla. He told us that we were all obliged to march in the festival's demonstration. He is also the Mayor of San Pedro and because everyone is scared of his relationship with the military, he can demand free labor from us for municipal works. On this occasion, he told the patrollers that we had to help build a municipal building without being paid."[59]

Patrol members from San Pedro Jocopilas and Chichicastenango reported that patrollers are forced to collect firewood for the civil patrol leaders and soldiers.[60]

(c). Control of freedom of movement.

In the northern areas of the Quiche province incidents have been reported of the civil patrols restricting citizens' freedom of movement. In the village of Xeciquel, for example, patrollers require that all men, women and children report to the patrol station before entering or leaving the village and report where they are going and how long they will be gone.[61]

(4). CONCLUSIONS.

The civil patrols are not voluntary neighborhood watch groups. The civil patrollers exert control over indigenous communities through threats and violence and they routinely commit human rights abuses. Civil patrollers coerce participation in the patrols, force the conscription of minors and murder, attack, and harass non-patrollers and human rights activists.

---

[58] *Interviews by author in 1991 and 1992 with residents of Xeciquel.*
[59] *Interview by the author with civil patrol member from San Pedro Jocopilas in Santa Cruz del Quiche on July 4, 1992.*
[60] *Interviews by the author with civil patrollers from San Pedro and Chichicastenango in July 1992.*
[61] *The author witnessed this incident in Xeciquel, May 8, 1992.*

V. THE MILITARY IS RESPONSIBLE FOR THE CIVIL PATROLS

(1). THE MILITARY ASSERTS THAT THE CIVIL PATROLS ARE INDEPENDENT, VOLUNTARY GROUPS, DENIES MILITARY ACCOUNTABILITY FOR THE PATFOLS AND DENIES THAT CIVIL PATROLLERS COMMIT HUMAN RIGHTS ABUSES.[62]

The military establishment rejects allegations by human rights groups that the civil patrols commit human rights violations, and denies that civil patrollers are the perpetrators of threats, attacks, and murders. The military commander of the Quiche base No. 20, Coronel Mario Terazzo Pinot, stated that complaints from the village of Tunaja were invented and that the community was "full of liars."[63]

Military officials assert that participation in the civil patrols is voluntary and that they are spontainiously organized groups formed to protect the communities from insurgent attacks.

Furthermore, army officials state that civil patrols are independent citizens' committees which seek military assistance, but for whom the military is not responsible. Military leaders disclaim accountability for the civil patrols, and their actions, whilst justifying their sponsorship of these groups as part of the armed forces constitutional obligation "to maintain internal security."[64] General Jose Garcia Samayoa, the Minister of Defense recently stated,

> "The self defense committees are non governmental organizations that have no relation with the army."[65]

(2). THE MILITARY IS REPONSIBLE FOR THE CIVIL PATROLS AND THEIR ACTIONS

The U.N. expert on Guatemala, Christian Tomuschat, confirms to the contrary that:

> "According to all available evidence, the armed forces have everywhere played a decisive role in creating the patrols, instructing them, and providing them partially with arms."[66]

---

[62] *These are positions stated during interviews by the RFK delelgation with General Jose Garcia Samayoa, (Minister of Defense) Captain Yon Rivera, (Director of the Department of Information of the Armed Forces), and Colonel Mario Terrazzo Pinot, (then Commander of the Quiche base No. 20) on June 12 and 14th 1991.*

[63] *Interview by the RFK delegation with Colonel Terrazzo, Santa Cruz del Quiche, June l4, 1992.*

[64] *Article 244 of the Constitution assigns the military protection of both internal and foreign security.*

[65] *See the article "Garcia Samayoa: Self Defense Groups Will Not Disappear," in the daily newspaper, "La Hora," on August 8, 1992.*

[66] *See the U.N. report, supra, paragraph 47.*

The military is legally and organizationally responsible for the civil patrol actions and accountable for their human rights violations. The military arms the civil patrols and regularly meets with civil patrollers to direct strategy.

Moreover, members of the armed forces commit human rights abuses which encourage civil patrollers to follow suit. They compel participation in the civil patrols and intimidate and threaten resisters. The military specifically target human rights activists who criticize the patrols, such as CERJ members and, most severely, human rights advocate Amilcar Mendez Urizar.

(a). The military arms the civil patrols:

The military establishment provides the civil patrols with arms. Usually these weapons are M-1 guns, M-15 guns or old rifles. Officials maintain that the patrollers must be armed to protect their communities from guerilla attacks training and bad weapons."

(b). The military is legally responsible for the civil patrols.

The Guatemalan armed forces are legally responsible for the civil patrols which serve as military reserve forces under the command of the Minister of Defense.[67] Decree 19-86 declares that:

> "Self-defense committees are recognized as organizations of civil nature and an expression of the Mobile and Territorial Reserves which . . . should be auxiliary forces coordinated by the Minister of Defense."[68]

However, the army does not provide sophisticated arms to the civil patrols and provides rudimentary training on the use of these weapons. The President of the Congressional Commission for the Indigenous Congress recently remarked that:

> "In theory they are supposed to defend the communities against subversion, but they could never do that with their lack of training and bad weapons."[69]

(c). The military is organizationally responsible for the civil patrols.

The military regularly meets with the civil patrol chiefs to discuss strategy, to regulate and supervise patrol activities, and to gain information about insurgents and dissidents. A civil patroller from San Pedro Jocopilas

---

[67] *See Decree 19-86, published on January 10, 1986.*
[68] *Decree 19-86, published January 10, 1986 in "Leyes emitidas durante et ano 1986," page 48.*
[69] *Interview by the author with Delegate Coxaj on August 25, 1992.*

describes the relationship between the civil patrollers and local military personnel as follows:

> "We have patrol meetings every fifteen days with all the patrollers. The chiefs and the military commissioners have meetings with the municipal chief of the patrols, Francisco Ixcoy, every eight days. They have to report about suspicious activities in the village so that Francisco can take that to his meetings with the army. They come back from meetings with orders from the military to control non-patrollers and members of human rights groups."[70]

The Inter American Commission of Human Rights for the Organization of American States describes the relationship between the military and the civil patrols as follows:

> "The patrols operate under the control of the local military command and a responsible person known as the *"comisionado"* [military commissioner]. Each of them also has a patrol chief designated in every locality by the military commander, who is required to report directly all events occurring in their jurisdiction. Members of the civil defense patrols receive continuous although rudimentary training... Aside from their usefulness as a shock force to prevent surprise attacks or counteract small insurgent assaults, their service is very useful to the government in providing reports of what goes on in their town... They act as the eyes and ears of the army... The three institutions [the civil patrollers, the patrol chiefs, and the military commissioners]... constitute the base of the military administrative pyramid... At the top, as the maximum authority responsible for the direction, coordination, control and execution, is the Chief of Staff of National Defense."[71]

(3). THE MILITARY COMPELS INDIGENOUS MEN TO PERFORM CIVIL PATROL DUTY.

Although military officials attempts to dismiss allegations that officials and soldiers harrass civilians to do patrol service, evidence proves that the military coerces indigenous men into the patrols. The commander of the military base in the Quiche province, Colonel Terrazzo, displayed records of petitions which the army claims to have received from communities requesting assistance to set up civil patrols. He insisted thatthis was all the proof

---

[70] *Interview by the author with a civil patroller, July 1992.*
[71] *This extract is quoted in an unpublished petition from CHRLA to the Inter American Commission of Human Rights, and is quoted from a report by the expert, Mr. Hector Gros Espiell, on Guatemala, prepared in accordance with paragraph 9 of Commission resolution 1989174, U.N. Document E/CN.411990145, at paragraphs 44 and 45.*

necessary to show that there was no forced membership.[72]

The fact that some communities request permission for civil patrols does not ensure that other patrols are voluntary. Equally, the signatories of the requests, the patrol chiefs, may not represent the popular preference. However, the requests do demonstrate that the army controls the civil patrols since the military can grant or deny the creation of each group of civil patrollers.

(a). Army officials assert that the civil patrol service is obligatory.

Officials and soldiers in the highlands continue to assert that patrol duty is obligatory.

> During 1991, according to a witness from a community in Chichicastenango, the army on at least four occasions instructed local men that patrolling was obligatory. In 1992, the army stayed in the town for fifteen days and told people they must do civil patrol service. Soldiers accused local men of being guerrillas if they refused to do their service.[73]

> Witnesses from a village in Totonicapan reported that military commissioners threatened local men to accept the position of new patrol commander. The commissioners held guns against the heads of the reluctant men and stated that participation in the civil patrols was obligatory. The commissioners added that if they refused, they were guerillas.[74]

(b). Army officials intimidate those who wish to withdraw from patrolling.

Dozens of communities in the Quiche area and in Huehuetenango have rejected civil patrol duties. The military consequently harasses and intimidates many of these communities. To generate support for the civil patrols, members of the army threaten a return to the savage violence of the early 1980's (in which the army burnt more than four hundred indigenous villages to the ground and massacred thousands of the residents), if civil patrols are terminated. Furthermore, the military labels opponents to the civil patrols system as pro-guerilla or as subversive. Men from three communities describe as follows their experiences with the military:

> In 1986, according to a witness from the Zacualpa area, the people in

---

[72] *RFK delegation interviews on June 12 and 14, 1992 with General Jose Samayoa, Captain Yon Rivera and Colonel Mario Rolando Terrazzo.*
[73] *Interview by CHRLA representative with a non-patroller in Santa Cruz del Quiche, July 20, 1992.*
[74] *See CERJ records, March 1, 1992.*

his community decided to terminate their civil patrol service. They approached the military garrison to report their decision, but the military refused to accept their petition and reiterated that they were obliged to patrol. A few days later, military officials and soldiers arrived in the community and instructed the men that they were required to patrol, but people stood fast by their decision. Since then, army officials have told other nearby villages that the people from this community are bad - that they are guerrillas.[75]

In 1988, the majority of men in a village in Santa Cruz del Quiche decided to terminate their patrol duty. According to a witness, appointed delegates went to tell the military officials about the decision. The official came back to the town and called a town meeting. He asked the people what they thought of those who wanted to quit. The people supported the delegates and only about seventy-five out of four hundred men said that they wanted to continue with the civil patrols. The official stated: "Those that do not want to do it are guerillas and they will bring back the violence that we experienced in 1981." The people got scared and, in the end, only ninety-five men maintained that they would no longer do service. After a month, the non-patrollers started receiving threats from the patrol members. They reported these incidents to the local office of the Ombudsman for Human Rights. The ombudsman called the patrollers in for questioning. When the accused presented themselves, they broke down and said: "We don't know what to do, because the law says we should not do this, but the army has told us to threaten and control non-patrollers."[76]

A resident from another community in Santa Cruz del Quiche stated that:

"On May 2, 1992, the army arrived in my town. Some soldiers were dressed in civilian clothing and others in green army uniforms. They called the civil patrollers together and said that all men had to patrol, as, if they did not, then the violence would return as it was in 1978, '79, '80, '81, the periods of most severe oppression."[77]

(c). Army officials threaten and detain those who have ceased patrolling.

The military attempts to eliminate lawful dissent and accuses non-patrollers of collaborating with the insurgency. The military frightens non-patrollers and encourages civil patrollers to operate through a campaign of intimidation.

---

[75] *Interview by the CHRLA representative with an ex-patroller in Santa Cruz del Quiche, July 3, 1992.*
[76] *Interview by the author with a non-patroller in Santa Cruz del Quiche on July 7, 1992.*
[77] *See CERJ records, May 4, 1992.*

In May, 1992, soldiers issued new guns to patrollers in San Pedro Jocopilas after some patrollers abandoned the civil patrol. The soldiers said that because of this action, the patrols needed the arms to protect the community more than ever from the insurgents.[78]

On June 3, 1992, a group of soldiers went to the seventeen villages of Chichicastenango, visited all the houses, and sought information about non-patrollers. They took down the names of non-patrollers and accused them of being guerillas who should be killed.[79]

Members of the community of Tunaja reported that since January, 1992 they have suffered a series of assaults and threats. They ascribed these assaults to having dissolved the civil patrol in January 1992. On January 19, 1992, Manuel Chingo de la Cruz was detained and kidnapped in Tunaja by soldiers from the military garrison in Zacualpa, Quiche and kept at the base until January 21st. The commander interrogated him during his detention, threatened him with a gun, and said he could not leave the garrison until he had given the army information about the guerrillas. Manuel's wife twice came to the base on January 20th to look for him, only to be told that he was not there. On January 21st, a group of about 150 people from the community demonstrated in front of the garrison and demanded Manuel's release. The army only then allowed Manuel to leave.[80]

(d). The army discriminates against non-patrollers in military conscription.

The army uses selective military recruitment as another method of social control of those individuals who oppose the civil patrols. During 1992, the army has discriminated against non-patrollers in military conscription in the Quiche area. Quiche is the one department in Guatemala where the army has begun to use legal methods in calling up men for the obligatory military service. In other regions, the army captures young men from buses, or rounds them up on market day. In Quiche, the military receives recruiting lists from a local draft committee which consists of civil patrol commanders, the mayor, and military commissioners. The military receives names of perceived dissenters.[81]

A witness describes the army's discriminatory conscription as follows:

---

[78] *See CERJ records of May 16, 1992.*
[79] *Interview by CHRLA with a non-patroller from Chichicastenango in July 1992.*
[80] *Interview by the RFK delegation with members of the Tunaja community on June 14, 1992.*
[81] *RFK delegation interview with members of the indigenous rights group, Maja Wil Q'ij (the "New Dawn") on June 13, 1992.*

In June 1992, the army visited all the villages in Chichicastenango and asked for the names of all the young men who did not patrol. They stated that they were going to use the list for military service recruitment. The army added that all the young men who refused to do civil patrol service were going to be called up before the rest of the men, and punished.[82]

(4). THE MILITARY REPRESSES HUMAN RIGHTS ORGANIZATIONS.

The routine attacks on human rights organizations and activists, such as the leaders and members of CERJ, illustrate the military's violent intolerance of independendent community organization. According to witnesses from Santa Cruz del Quiche, the military commissioner stated that he was disturbed by any organizing activity, whether for CERJ or for simple cultural activities.[83] In highland Guatemala, the army principally targets organizations such as CERJ which oppose the civil patrol service. Congressman Peter H. Kostmayer stated that:

> "The [military] high command supports a limited concept of democracy that ... does not include an effective right to organize to achieve political objectives."[84]

(a). The military conducts a disinformation campaign against CERJ.

Members of the military routinely label and link CERJ and its leaders to the insurgents. The military maintains a campaign of vilification to discredit CERJ and to portray the organization as opponents of peace.

> On June 11, 1992, Francisco Ixcoy, the municipal leader of the civil patrols, called together seven communities of San Pedro Jocopilas to meet with Captain Gordon Pais, the head of the army's civil affairs division from the military base No. 20 in Quiche. Captain Pais stated that "CERJ and other human rights groups are liars and make false denouncements. These groups are never going to beat us, we are going to crush them, therefore you should all join us against these groups. The leaders and members of these groups are subversives."[85]

---

[82] *CHRLA interviews with three witnesses from different communities of the municipality of Chichicastenango, on July 3, 6, and 7, 1992.*
[83] *Delegation meeting with CERJ members on June 14, 1992 in Santa Cruz del Quiche.*
[84] *Statement by Congressman Kostmayer to the Sub-Committee on Western Hemispheric Affairs on July 17, 1992.*
[85] *Interview by the author with a witness from San Pedro Jocopilas on July 4, 1992.*

A civil patroller from Parraxtut reported that:

On March 4, 1992, the military arrived in Parraxtut and called a meeting with the civil patrollers and military commissioners. Members of CERJ were pointed out during the meeting and an army official stated that: "Those who are members of human rights groups are part of the guerrillas. The patrollers must control these people's houses at night to see if there is any strange activity."[86]

(b). The military attacks Amilcar Mendez Urizar.

Human rights advocates like CERJ leader Amilcar Mendez Urizar are persistently threatened and attacked by the military. During 1992, the military openly targeted and maligned Mendez and his work. Mendez continues to endure vicious and life-threatening attacks, including a recent bomb attack on his house.

On May 10, 1992, at 10:10 pm, a hand grenade exploded against the outer wall of Mendez' house in Santa Cruz del Quiche. Although Mendez was not at home at the time, his brother, Ariel Mendez, and his brother's family were inside the house. The police, the local Human Rights Ombudsman, and Colonel Terazzo from the Quiche army base arrived at the scene within minutes of the attack. The police recovered a piece of the grenade.

Two days later, Captain Yon Rivera, head of the military's Department of Information, stated during a press conference that the incident seemed a bit strange, because police had received a call from a Professor Mendez prior to the grenade explosion, stating that the attack was about to take place.

Captain Yon Rivera's statement was widely interpreted to imply that Amilcar Mendez had staged the event.

When asked about his statement, Captain Yon Rivera subsequently stated that he was only repeating what the police had told him.[87] The police, however, denied ever reporting this information to the military Department of Information. The local Quiche police claimed that they had received only one call, three minutes after the incident, from Ariel Mendez.[88]

---

[86] *Interview by the author with CERJ members from Parraxtut, Santa Cruz del Quiche on March 6, 1992.*

[87] *RFK delegation meeting with Yon Rivera in Santa Cruz del Quiche in June 1992.*

[88] *Interview by the author with the Chief of Police in Santa Cruz del Quiche on May 12, 1992.*

Colonel Terrazzo denied the allegation that the report that "Professor Mendez" had given a warning prior of the impending explosion had originated from him. He denied that the military was at all involved in the incident.[88] During an interview about the bomb attack, Colonel Terrazzo revealed the serial number allegedly found on the grenade, displayed boxes of grenades and a large list of serial numbers of grenades from the base, none of which matched the number of the explosive used.[90]

Captain Yon Rivera agreed to issue a statement that the military supports the work of CERJ and that any threat against CERJ was equal to a threat against the military.[91] To date, no such statement has been issued. Instead, disinformation followed.

Two months after the bomb attack, the Guatemalan military insinuated that Amilcar Mendez was involved in a homicide where his brother, Marvin Mendez Urizar, stood accused. Amilcar Mendez denies any involvement in this incident.

Marvin Mendez is accused of having killed Felipe Reyes Alvarez on July 26, 1992. According to eyewitness accounts, Felipe Reyes attacked Marvin Mendez with a machete. Marvin Mendez threw a rock at Felipe Reyes to protect himself from Reyes' machete, and the rock struck Reyes in the chest. Reyes died within minutes. On July 28th, two days after the incident, army helicopters flew journalists to the Reyes' funeral in San Andres Sacabaja. According to witnesses, military officials alleged that Amilcar Mendez had been involved in the crime.

In a press statement four days later, Captain Yon Rivera accused Amilcar Mendez of helping his brother to escape from the law.[92]

On July 29, 1992 Colonel Terrazzo and Captain Gordon Pais, the head of the army's civil affairs division at the Quiche base, called a community meeting in San Pedro Jocopilas. They allegedly told the community that Amilcar Mendez had ordered his brother to kill Reyes.[93]

On July 31, pamphlets were distributed in the streets of Santa Cruz del Quiche. The pamphlets depicted cartoons of a man killing another man, and read: "Murderous CERJ...Where are human rights?" The pamphlets were signed by the "Patriotic Christian Front," which had previously appeared on smear pamphlets about CERJ.

---

[89] *Interview by the author with Colonel Terrazzo on May 12, 1992.*
[90] *Author's meeting with Colonel Terrazzo on May 12, 1992.*
[91] *RFK delegation meeting with Captain Yon Rivera in Guatemala City on June 15, 1992.*
[92] *See report in the daily newspaper, "La Hora," July 30, 1992.*
[93] *Interview by the author with witness from San Pedro Jocopilas on August 2, 1992.*

On August 2, 1992, Francisco Ixcoy, the municipal patrol commander in San Pedro Jocopilas, ordered civil patrollers to appear at a town meeting the following day. Ixcoy then instructed everyone present to attend a demonstration to condemn Mendez in Santa Cruz del Quiche.[94] About five hundred patrollers attended the demonstration and shouted: "Amilcar Mendez and CERJ pretend to be leaders for human rights. Instead of applying the law, they kill humble peasants."

On August 5, Captain Yon Rivera again attacked Amilcar Mendez in a press statement which referred to: "bad, resentful Guatemalans who discredit their country only so that they can gain comfortable positions in life, pretending to monitor human rights and the well being of their compatriots, whom they actually treat with arrogance."[95]

Military involvement in a civilian or criminal case such as this case, is questionable and unacceptable, especially where the military is determined to discredit human rights advocates such as Amilar Mendez by linking Mendez to alleged criminal behavior.

(5). CONCLUSIONS.

The military organized the civil patrols during the 1980's as a counterinsurgency measure and to extend and consolidate military control over the rural highlands. Today, the civil patrols continue to be used as auxiliary forces of the military, to weed out dissent and to secure military dominance in the rural communities. The civil patrols enforce the army's strategy and the military exercise control by proxy while disclaiming accountability for human rights abuses which civil patrollers commit.

However, as Guatemalan Congressman Claudio Coxaj recently stated:

> "There are two kinds of responsibility for [civil patrol] crimes. One is *"del hecho"* [of the act] and the other is *"asesoria intelectual"* [intellectual assistance]. The latter is from the armed forces and they are responsible for the education of the civil patrols."[96]

The military is legally and organizationally responsible for the civil patrols and is accountable for human rights violations committed by civil patrollers. Members of the military persecute non-patrollers and human rights activists and so encourage the impunity of the military and of the civil patrollers.

---

[94] *Interview by the author with patroller from San Pedro Jocopilas on August 2, 1992.*
[95] *See report in the daily newspaper "Prensa Libre," August 5, 1992.*
[96] *Author's interview with Congressionai Delegate Claudio Coxaj on August 25, 1991.*

VI. THE GOVERNMENT IS RESPONSIBLE FOR THE CIVIL PATROLS AND FOR HUMAN RIGHTS ABUSES.

(1). PRESIDENT SERRANO PROMISES REFORM AND TO UPHOLD HUMAN RIGHTS.

When he was elected in 1991, President Serrano promised to end Guatemala's horrendous human rights record and the impunity of violators of human rights. The government today asserts that it vigilantly safeguards human rights and especially created governmental human rights institutions to that end. Government officials claim that special protections and support are given to human rights activists.

President Serrano's promises of reform and justice remain unfulfilled. President Serrano himself attacks human rights activists as collaborators with the guerrillas. Moreover, the government tolerates routine human rights abuses committed by the military, by "paramilitary" groups and by the civil patrols. Government human rights institutions (such as the Coordinating Commission for Executive Policy in Respect of Human Rights, the Congress Human Rights Committee, and the Office of the Human Rights Ombudsman), created to further encourage respect for human rights, are not capable of fulfilling their limited mandates.

The government echoes military claims that the civil patrols are voluntary, independent community watch groups which guard the communities against the insurgency and crime. The government has not terminated the military's impunity and dominance over civil authorities in the highlands of Guatemala. The justice system routinely fails to provide redress for crimes committed by the military or civil patrollers.

(2). PRESIDENT SERRANO ACCUSES AMILCAR MENDEZ URIZAR OF WORKING WITH THE INSURGENCY.

The Guatemalan government threatens human rights advocates and human rights groups in Guatemala by branding them as supportive of the guerrillas. President Serrano commented publicly in Washington, D.C. on September 30, 1991 that:

> "Mendez is working with the insurrection. We have documented all his relations with them... CERJ is a parallel organization to the insurgency."[97]

When President Serrano was asked by representatives of U.S. human rights groups for such evidence, he replied that Mendez was very active in the Quiche area and that CERJ used the same slogans as the guerrilla groups. He also

---

[97] *The President made this statement in Washington D.C. at the Carnegie Institute for Peace.*

declared that he had documents with him which proved his statement, but failed to produce any such documents.

On December 11, 1991, Mendez, his family and other CERJ leaders met with President Serrano to seek an explanation for his remarks. They first met with Bernardo Neumann, President of COPREDEH, who denied that Serrano had ever made these remarks.[98] At that moment, the President walked in and confirmed his statement in Washington that Mendez and CERJ worked parallel with the guerrillas and stated that he would repeat it. On January 13, 1992, he again alleged in his annual address that he had evidence of Mendez's collaboration with the guerrillas. To date, President Serrano has not once revoked his words.

President Serrano's statements about Mendez and CERJ function as a license to kill. Such statements encourage those responsible for previous attacks against Mr. Mendez and CERJ to continue their campaign. A Guatemalan journalist reported that "it is the same as putting him [Mendez] in front of the barrel of a gun."[99]

Since the remarks by President Serrano, Mendez and CERJ have suffered more severe attacks, threats and harassment. Statements linking human rights advocates to guerrilla groups mirror strategies used by the civil patrols, the military and paramilitary death squads to legitimize repression of lawful opposition to military control.

(3). THE GOVERNMENT TOLERATES HUMAN RIGHTS VIOLATIONS.

(a). The government human rights institutions fail to adequately protect human rights.

The Government claims that it is providing protection to its citizens and specifically to CERJ members and Amilcar Mendez. Officials claim that three government human rights agencies adequately monitor the human rights situation: COPREDEH advises the President about human rights in Guatemala; the Congressional Human Rights Committee monitors human rights for the legislature; and the office of the Ombudsman for Human Rights investigates human rights cases, but does not have the power to initiate prosecutions against human rights violators.

The Presidential Coordinating Commission for Executive Policy in respect of Human Rights ("COPREDEH") coordinates activities of the executive's ministries and institutions with those of the judiciary and the Ombudsman for Human Rights, and it promotes the investigation of complaints about human rights abuses.

---

[98] *When the RFK delegation met with Bernardo Neumann, he stated that the President had been misunderstood.*

[99] *See report by Carlo Rafael Soto in the daily newspaper "El Grafico," January 9, 1992.*

COPREDEH does not fulfill its investigative role. COPREDEH stated in its most recent report that:

> "Mr. Mendez has been offered protection and guarantees, which he has not accepted. In addition, all of the relevant institutions and government agencies have expressed their readiness to assist him."[100]

Amilcar Mendez maintains that the only protection provided by the government was the placement of a policeman at his house in Santa Cruz del Quiche. Mr. Hurtado Prem, then Minister of the Interior, on one occasion told Mendez that he could provide him with permanent police escorts. Although the police presence is a positive development, such action alone does not discharge the Government's obligations to protect Mendez and members of CERJ.

The Congressional Commission for Human Rights was created in terms of Article 263 of the Guatemalan Constitution. Enabling legislation provided that the Commission could study and propose legislative initiatives involving human rights; hold seminars investigating human rights; elect the Ombudsman for Human Rights and mediate between that office and members of the Congress; submit recommendations about human rights to state agencies; maintain constant communication with national and international human rights organizations; study international complaints about human rights in Guatemala and refer such complaints to the Ombudsman for Human Rights.

Although the Congressional Commission for Human Rights has received many complaints from human rights groups about the civil patrol's human rights violations, no legislative action has been taken to respond to these complaints.

The office of the Ombudsman for Human Rights was established in 1986. Within the jurisdiction of the Ombudsman lie both constitutionally guaranteed rights and rights protected by international human rights laws. As such, this office has the widest mandate of the three government human rights institutions. It may receive complaints about human rights violations, conduct investigations, file complaints with the court, and recommend prosecution of human rights violators. The Ombudsman may report human rights violations and submit recommendations about human rights to the government. However, the function of this office to promote and protect human rights is limited, because the Ombudsman cannot pursue prosecutions.

The Ombudsman's office demonstrates a commitment to challenge the impunity of the civil patrols, but falls short of fulfilling its mandate. The efforts of the Ombudsman have been dedicated mostly to reporting human rights violations. Efforts of thorough and independent investigation in the highlands of Guatemala are foiled by the obstructive and dominating military authority.

Civil patrollers have attacked representatives from the office of the Human

---

[100] *COPREDEH Report on the Human Rights Situation in Guatemala from January 1 to April 30, 1992.*

Rights Ombudsman. The Adjunct Ombudsman, Cesar Alvarez Guademuz, has survived six or seven attempts on his life. The most infamous incident took place when civil patrollers from Parraxtut, Sacapulas shot at him in April 1990.[101] More recently, on June 6, 1991, the regional Ombudsman from Quiche, Oscar Cifuentes, was investigating an illegal arrest by civil patrollers in Chiul, Cunen, when he had to flee the town before investigating the situation. When he attempted to hold a public meeting, hundreds of civil patrollers shouted that he was a guerrilla, because he worked in human rights. They also threw stones at his car as he escaped.[102]

The three government human rights institutions lack both the authority and the jurisdiction to challenge the power and impunity of the military establishment and the civil patrols. By not fully investigating human rights abuses, relief to victims remains limited and ineffective, and attacks against human rights advocates continue.

(b). The Government tolerates "paramilitary" intimidation against Amilcar Mendez and CERJ.

Members and leaders of CERJ are routinely subjected to a barrage of defamatory material, attacks and intimidation by paramilitary groups, which also carry out extrajudicial executions. Human rights organizations and community groups in Guatemala widely believe that these threats and slanderous propaganda originate from the security forces, even when pamphlets are signed by right-wing paramilitary groups. The army denies any involvement in the campaign against CERJ and thus dodges accountability. Human rights groups consider it a tactic of the armed forces to publicly discredit and destroy support for CERJ and to frighten CERJ leaders and members. The Government effectively encourages violence against CERJ by allowing such attacks and intimidation to continue without investigation or condemnation.

(i). Assaults against Mendez.

Amilcar Mendez has survived physical attacks from assailants. On April 15, 1991, Mendez was assaulted by four men in dark glasses outside a restaurant on Avenida Roosevelt in Guatemala City. Two assailants tried to grab him, but he screamed, and a passerby fortunately intervened. The assailants fled and one of them shouted that Mendez was going to die.

(ii). Written death threats to Mendez.

Mendez has also received numerous death threats from paramilitary groups in Guatemala since President Serrano began his term:

---

[101] *For detail about other incidents, see the Americas Watch report, "Guatemala: Army Campaign Against Human Rights Activists Intensifies," May 1990.*

[102] *Testimony from a video filmed at the meeting and interviews by author with witnesses, August 1991.*

In August 1991, Mendez received a death threat in a letter from a paramilitary group, *Jaguar Justiciero*, a group renowned for violent and repressive acts against students and union leaders.[103] The letter alleged that Mr. Mendez is aiding the insurgent URNG and that he will die.[104]

In June 1992, the renowned death squad *Unidad Anticommunista* ("Anti-communist Unity") issued death threats to various popular leaders. The name of Amilcar Mendez headed the list.

These attacks remain uninvestigated by the government. By tolerating such acts, the government encourages the impunity of the paramilitary groups and further endangers Mendez's security.

(iii). Circulation of defamatory material against Mendez and CERJ.

Anti-CERJ pamphlets and flyers are regularly distributed as part of an increasingly popular form of propaganda against Mendez and CERJ.

Throughout October and November 1990, soon after Mendez had received the Robert F. Kennedy Human Rights Award, pamphlets were distributed on busy market days in Santa Cruz del Quiche, where CERJ has its main office. The pamphlets were signed by *El Movimiento Indigena Utatllan* ("The Indigenous Utatlan Movement"). Some pamphlets alleged that CERJ was responsible for killing and dividing the Quiche people. Other pamphlets stated that Mendez had won a lot of money and was now going to flee the country.[105]

In December, 1991, more pamphlets were distributed to CERJ members in Chunima, Chichicastenango, a community where three CERJ members have been killed since October 1990. The pamphlets were signed by the *Frente Patriotica Cristiana* ("The Christian Patriotic Front"). One of the pamphlets alleged that Mendez had fled the country because of a warrant for his arrest for violating human rights. Another pamphlet accused CERJ and other popular groups of being members of the URNG guerrilla group and of being responsible for crimes against the Quiche people.

In January and February 1992, more pamphlets were distributed in Santa Cruz del Quiche, depicting Mendez fleeing the country with bags

---

[103] For other incidents see Americas Watch report, "Messengers of Death, Human Rights in Guatemala," November 1988-February 1990, page 19.
[104] A copy of this letter is attached as appendix 2 to this report.
[105] See appendix 3 to this report.

of money while leaving behind a starving CERJ member. Another pamphlet alleged that Mendez had accused a minor of kidnapping a CERJ member.[106]

This campaign of vilification and intimidation against Mendez does not end at the Guatemalan borders. During September to November 1991, Mendez and his family sought temporary refuge in the United States as a consequence of these continuous attacks. On October 15, 1991, Mendez attended a luncheon sponsored by the RFK Center and the Washington Office on Latin America in Washington D.C. During the luncheon, an unknown person left a stack of defamatory pamphlets in the building. The pamphlet contained photos of Mendez with President Serrano and linked Mendez to guerrilla groups.[107]

The government has not investigated any of these incidents or prosecuted offenders who continue to attack the human rights community in Guatemala.

(4). THE ADMINISTRATION OF JUSTICE IN THE HIGHLANDS OF GUATEMALA HAS FAILED.

The judiciary has proved to be ineffective in upholding the law in rural Guatemala.[108] As Christian Tomuschat reported in 1991:

"Only the victims, not the perpetrators, can be accounted for."[109]

Adequate mechanisms exist to protect citizens' rights through the constitution, legislation, the formal institutions of justice, and the international treaties which the Guatemalan government has ratified. These international human rights treaties confirm the obligation of the Guatemalan government to uphold the rule of law and due process.

Hence, the military and the civil patrols dominate civil authorities in rural Guatemala. As the U.S. Department of State reported in 1991:

"The security forces are virtually never held accountable for human rights violations . . . civil patrol leaders enjoy army backing and virtual *de facto* immunity from prosecution."[110]

Guatemalans understandably lack confidence in the administration of justice, which rarely produces relief to the victims of human rights violations. The civil patrols act in contempt of the law, thwart the judicial process, and fortify

---

[106] *See appendices 4 and 5.*
[107] *See appendix 9.*
[108] *For a full account of the Guatemalan system of justice and human rights before President Serrano came to power, see Kenneth Anderson's report for the International Human Rights Law Group, "Maximizing Deniability: The Justice System and Human Rights in Guatemala," of July 1989.*
[109] *See the U.N. report by Tomuschat, supra, paragraph 83.*
[110] *See USDOS 1991 Report, supra.*

the control of the military. To challenge the civil patrols invites retaliation, and overwhelming fear of retribution prevents victims from prosecuting offenders, witnesses from testifying and judges from pursuing human rights cases.

The absence of justice for victims of human rights abuses can be directly traced to the flawed Guatemalan justice system and to the Serrano government's failure to uphold the law, to protect human rights, and to root out the impunity of the Guatemalan armed forces and the civil patrols. In 1990, Harvard University canceled its support program for the Guatemalan judiciary. The Harvard team indicated that their efforts were wasted in the context of complete disrespect for human rights and lack of political will by the Government to change it.[111]

(a). The judiciary fails to protect human rights.

Judges in Guatemala miserably fail to protect the rights of Guatemala's indigenous population. Since CERJ was founded in 1988, the group has filed over four hundred *habeas corpus* applications or complaints seeking the investigation and prosecution of civil patrollers who have violated human rights. The majority of these cases remain in *sobre averiguar* ("under investigation"): often the police have not identified witnesses, and judges have not prosecuted the culprits.

(i). The habeas corpus remedy fails.

Although the Guatemalan Constitution establishes the substantial remedy of *habeas corpus* in Article 263, the judiciary has not implemented this remedy, especially in human rights cases and where the military or civil patrols are implicated. In none of the *habeas corpus* cases filed by CERJ for men who were illegally captured to render military service has the judge called on the military base in question to demand the release of the detainees. The following cases illustrate the disappearance of two CERJ members, and the response of the judiciary under the Serrano administration. None of the families has been informed of any judicial action taken to find the victims.

> Miguel Toj filed a *habeas corpus* application for his son, Santos Toj Reynoso, on June 2, 1991 with the Attorney General, the President of the Judiciary, and the Justice of the Peace in Santa Cruz del Quiche. He has received no report about any judicial investigation into the disappearance of his son.
>
> Amilcar Mendez Urizar filed a *habeas corpus* application for Esteban Tojin on May 29, 1992 with the investigating judge in the judiciary

---

[111] *Congressional testimony by Philip Heyman, Director of the Harvard Program, to the U.S. government's Congressional Sub-Committee on Western Hemispheric Affairs, July 17, 1990.*

morgue in Guatemala City. To date, no information about this case has been made available.[112]

Attempts by Amilcar Mendez to seek redress for threats have also been met with failure:

> On January 21, 1992, Amilcar Mendez filed with the President of the Supreme Court *habeas corpus* applications against President Serrano, stating that he feared for his life after President Serrano's repeated accusations that Mendez was working with the guerrillas. On January 22, 1992 the *Sala Tercera* of the appeals court issued a ruling that they could not continue with the judicial process because Mendez had not precisely described the respondents of the *habeas corpus* application. On January 28, 1992 Mendez appealed this ruling and stated that the previous petition had clearly named the President of Guatemala as the respondent and the culprit. Mendez asserted that the *Sala's* resolution was unnecessary and obstructive because the *habeas corpus* remedies clearly provide that it is not necessary to indicate against whom the petition is filed in cases of this nature. On January 29, 1992 the *Sala* referred the case to the Supreme Court. On February 26, 1992 the Supreme Court ruled that Mendez was not imprisoned, detained or restrained in any way from enjoying his right to individual liberty and there was no threat that Mendez could lose this liberty. The case therefore did not meet the requirements for the application of the law of *habeas corpus* remedy. On March 4, 1992 Amilcar Mendez appealed the decision, but his appeal was summarily rejected on March 5, 1992.

(ii). Assassinations are not investigated.

CERJ has reported twenty-five cases of assassinations or disappearances of CERJ members to the judiciary. In only three of these cases have the accused been arrested, including in the case relating to the assassination of Jose Maria Ixcaya on May 1, 1990; the assassination of Maria Mejia on March 17, 1990; and the assassinations of Juan Perebal Xirum and Manuel Perebal Morales on February 17, 1991. The alleged perpetrators in the Ixcaya and Mejia cases were, however, only held for fifteen days. Only the Perebal case proceeded to trial and the accused, Manuel Perebal Ajtzalam and Manuel Leon Lares, were acquitted by the Judge of the first instance in Santa Cruz del Quiche on June 15, 1992.

The experience of victims in San Pedro Jocopilas illustrates the failure of the judges to investigate, prosecute and convict assassins. In San Pedro Jocopilas, seven non-patrollers have been killed since 1990 and several complaints have been filed against the civil patrollers. No warrants for arrests were issued, and

---

[112] *Interviews by author with Amilcar Mendez, August 1992.*

no prosecutions or convictions ensued, as is illustrated by the following incidents:

On May 16, 1989, Marcelina Calel Lopez filed a complaint with the Ombudsman for Human Rights in Santa Cruz del Quiche, that her son, Miguel Tzoy Calel, was receiving death threats from Miguel Barrera Calel, the leader of the civil patrols in her village Santabal I in San Pedro Jocopilas. Barrera had said to her son that he must return to his civil patrol duty or "something bad would happen to him." No investigation followed her complaint. On April 19, 1991, her son was killed. She reported the assassination to the local Human Rights Ombudsman, but no investigation or prosecution has followed.[113]

On April 10, 1991, Jose Vicente Garcia, a very active CERJ member and a non-patroller, was killed in San Pedro Jocopilas. He had received death threats before his murder, but he had not filed a formal complaint about these threats.[114] His wife, Juana Sarat Ixcoy, and his mother-in-law, Katarina Ixcoy, witnessed his assassination. On April 11, 1991, Juana Sarat Ixcoy filed a complaint with the Ombudsman seeking an investigation into her husband's assassination. The two eyewitnesses have never been called in for questioning and no culprit has been detained or charged.[115]

On March 27, 1991, Juan Ajiataz Chivalan filed a complaint with the local Ombudsman for Human Rights and demanded an investigation into the murder of his two sons, Pablo Ajiataz Chivalan and Manuel Ajiataz Chivalan. His sons were assassinated in Santabal I in San Pedro Jocopilas on March 15, 1991. On April 11, 1991, he repeated his complaint in another petition to the Ombudsman, ratifying his last complaint and again appealing for an investigation. He demanded that the civil patrollers of his village Xoljuyub be questioned, because "they have such tight control of the town that they would have known who killed my boys." No on-site investigation has taken place and no civil patrollers have been called in for questioning.[116]

On July 1, 1991, Marcos Julaj Vicente filed a complaint with the Ombudsman for Human Rights in Quiche about the assassination of his brother, Celestino Julaj Vicente on June 28, 1991. His brother had allegedly received death threats from the civil patrol leader of the

---

[113] *Petitions to Procuradoria de los Derechos Humanos, April 4, 1991, and May 16, 1989.*
[114] *Interview by author with Garcia's mother, Santa Zapeta Garcia, July 4, 1992.*
[115] *Interview by author with Katarina Ixcoy, July 4, 1992.*
[116] *Interview by author with Amilcar Mendez, June 1992.*

village Chutzalic, Pedro Lopez Ajiataz, after he had become a member of CERJ and had terminated his patrol service on October 3, 1988. On July 15, 1991, Maria Lolmet Xom, Celestino's wife, who witnessed the assassination, was called into the Ombudsman's office to ratify Marcos' complaint and to make a statement. She did not recognize the alleged assassin, but accused the civil patrollers from their village as the intellectual authors of his death, because they had constantly threatened her husband as a CERJ member. No further investigation has followed.[117]

On August 26, 1992, Catarino Chanchavac Larios was killed. On August 31, 1992, his family members and non-patrollers from six of the villages around San Pedro Jocopilas filed a petition to the Human Rights Ombudsman in Quiche about his assassination and about the ongoing repression which non-patrollers face. They reported that they had filed numerous complaints with the Human Rights Ombudsman in recent years without any results and had called for an immediate investigation into all the reported killings. To date, no investigation has followed their complaints.[118]

(b). The judicial system is flawed.

The judiciary is inefficient and impeded by an archaic penal code. Judges are underpaid and corruption is a central problem to the criminal justice system.[119]

The work of the judiciary is complicated because of the double role of judges under Guatemala's Napoleonic judicial system, and because of an excessive reliance on written, closed non-public trials. Judges investigate crimes and decide in a pretrial procedure whether or not prosecution and a trial should follow. This practice allows for obstruction of the justice process, especially when the trial is quashed at the outset. Dr. Philip Heyman, director of the Center for Criminal Justice at Harvard University Law School, describes the pretrial procedure as follows:

> "Staff for courts call in witnesses and type up summaries of the answers to questions the staff ask under some limited supervision from the judge. Then, at the end of the investigative stage, if there is enough evidence to warrant this step, the file is sent to a trial judge. Tradition

---

[117] *See petitions filed with the office of the Human Rights Ombudsman, June 1, 1991, and June 15, 1991.*

[118] *See petition filed with the Ombudsman in Santa Cruz del Quiche, August 31, 1992.*

[119] *According to the Vice President of the Congressional Commission for Human Rights, Mr. Oscar Villar Anleu, at the time of writing this report, judges at the Santa Cruz del Quiche court are under investigation for corruption.*

ally the trial judge would, in perhaps eighty percent of the cases, simply read the written statements and render a verdict without ever seeing or personally speaking to the defendant, witnesses, and victims."[120]

Without open trials and access to the courts, suspicion and cynicism reign in the public. This is especially true among members of the indigenous communities, with their different traditions and languages.

Two features of the criminal justice system (described below) deserve specific scrutiny, because these provisions limit the jurisdiction of the judiciary to investigate abuses and to protect human rights.

Antejuicio grants government officials, members of congress, mayors, judges, and military commanders a special trial in an independent tribunal which decides whether sufficient evidence exists for prosecution.[121]

The other privilege, which interferes with the judiciary's capacity to protect human rights, provides that members of the armed forces are subject only to the jurisdiction of military tribunals. Christian Tomuschat describes these tribunals as follows:

> "Jurisdiction is exclusively vested in officers or special institutions of the armed forces. A court martial, the main body for judging criminal offenses committed by soldiers, is made up of five officers, none of whom may have had any legal training. In all proceedings under the system of military justice, an *auditor de guerra* who must be a lawyer with all the qualifications needed for a judge of first instance, advises the judicial institution concerned, but he himself is not a member of such institution. He takes part in the deliberations, but has no vote."[122]

This preferential treatment of the military effectively obliterates the fair and independent prosecution of military personnel for human rights violations perpetrated by the military officials, soldiers, or military commissioners. Even if civil patrollers are arrested and prosecuted, the intellectual authors of human rights violations often remain at large.[123] Guatemalan Congressman Claudio Coxaj summarizes the problem:

---

[120] *See statement by Philip Heyman to the U.S. government's Congressional SubCommittee on Western Hemispheric Affairs of the Committee on Foreign Affairs on July 17, 1990.*

[121] *See article 206 of the Guatemalan Constitution.*

[122] *See page 11 of Tomuschat report.*

[123] *There is no plea bargaining system in Guatemala. There may be less incentive to name the intellectual authors of crimes, given the weak guarantees for witness protection.*

> "I think all over the world when there are acts of violence, the weakest are punished and the most powerful wash their hands of responsibility."[124]

Government officials ascribe these problems with the judicial system as responsible for the failure of the administration of justice in Guatemala. They assert that proposed amendments to the Penal Code, the Military Code and the Code of Criminal Procedure, pending in Congress, will correct such historic problems. These proposed amendments will not guarantee an end to the impunity enjoyed by the armed forces and the civil patrollers. The military's domination of civil authorities in the highlands and the military's disregard for the rule of law remain the central problem to achieving justice and redress for victims of human rights violations in Guatemala.

(c). Civil patrols are the dominant rural authority.

The Serrano government tolerates and condones human rights violations by the security forces and the civil patrols. The Government is unwilling to admit that the military or the Government is responsible for the civil patrols. The government repudiates charges that the participation in the civil patrols is forced by the civil patrollers and their military sponsors. Manuel Conde Orellana, who leads the government's delegation in the peace negotiations, recently stated that:

> "The government is sure that the civil patrols, at the present time, function voluntarily."[125]

Government officials oppose the abolition of the civil patrols as unconstitutional. They insist that the provisions of Article 34 of the Constitution ensure freedom of association and self-defense to civilians.

Government officials assert that violence by the civil patrollers is inevitable and avoid questions about such violations. The government's Attorney General, Acisclo Valladares, contends that violence is unavoidable in a war situation. He recently stated that:

> "I am not surprised that there are cases of death threats against men who do not patrol, because they are living in a war zone."[126]

Bernardo Neumann (President of COPREDEH) stated that ninety-five per-

---

[124] *Interview by author with Vice President of the Congressional Commission for Human Rights, Oscar Villar Anleu, August 26, 1992.*
[125] *See report in "El Grafico" on August 9, 1992.*
[126] *Interview by the author with Attorney General Acisclo Valladares on August 25, 1992.*

cent of human rights violations were a result of the war.[127] The Vice President of the Congressional Commission for Human Rights, Oscar Anleu, alleged that the violence occurred as a result of private conflicts or feuds and not because of a military strategy.[128]

Such statements reveal that the government effectively encourages military control of the indigenous communities and sanctions military and civil patrol impunity.

Endorsed by the government, the civil patrols serve as the dominant authority in the highlands of Guatemala. Although a system of civil government exists in most of rural Guatemala, the military still wields preeminent power. Dr. Philip Heyman, the director of the Harvard Center for Criminal Justice support program in Guatemala, described the situation as follows:

> "The countryside is a place where to a large extent the military rule and where military violence against those who are suspected of being subversives or encouraging opposition to the military's antisubversive measures is commonplace and uninvestigated."[129]

Governors in the departmental capitals, mayors in the towns, and auxiliary mayors in each small community yield to the military's clout, exerted through the military officials and commissioners and civil patrol leaders. The communities generally lack respect for and confidence in the elected authorities. The International Human Rights Law Group describes military control as follows:

> "[A municipal worker remarked that] people did not care whether they had civilian mayors or not, because civilian mayors alone could not protect them from the army. His colleague, the chief municipal clerk... went even further. "The people are afraid," he said, "that what went on before will happen again... so they always want to know that whatever they do has been approved by the Army. That's why the people look to the civil patrol chief. He is the Army."[130]

(d). The civil patrols supersede the justice system.

Judicial structures in rural areas have been overpowered and violence, intimidation, and lawlessness reign. In many areas, civil patrols have taken control. As Robert Carmack, an anthropologist, recently wrote:

---

[127] *Interview by the RFK Center's delegation with Bernardo Neumann on June 12, 1992.*

[128] *Interview by author with Oscar Anleu on August 26, 1992.*

[129] *See the statement by Dr. Philip Heyman to the U.S. government's Congressional Sub-Committee on Western Hemispheric Affairs on July 17, 1990, page 7.*

[130] *See the report by the International Human Rights Law Group, "Maximizing Deniability," pages 49-50.*

"One of the features of the patrol system is that it replaced the national judicial system as an institution to solve conflicts and local disputes. In the past people went before the mayor, who took the place of a justice of peace or went before a higher judge in a departmental capital to solve differences or denounce personal damages or crimes . . . But by 1985, there was virtually no judicial system in the Indian rural communities, and most of the disputes were solved by violent acts of the local civil patrol commandants, or at the last instance by local or regional commandants of the army itself."[131]

(e). The civil patrollers interfere with judicial proceedings.

Victims, witnesses and judges are persecuted for challenging abuse by the civil patrollers. Victims are hesitant to initiate judicial proceedings, because filing petitions and demanding respect for human rights often result in persecution, not justice. Fear of retaliation intimidates witnesses into not taking legal action or coming forward to testify. In general, judges are reluctant to pursue human rights cases for the same reason. The following examples illustrate the military and civil patrol domination over justice in rural Guatemala.

(i). Witnesses and victims are persecuted.

The government fails to provide adequate protection for witnesses and for victims of human rights abuses. Witness protection is completely absent and civilians fear the criminal justice system because of retribution. The government's failure to provide such protection diminishes the basic rights to justice and equal protection under the law for victims of human rights violations. The following examples (a few among hundreds of similar cases) reveal the persecution suffered by victims and by witnesses who demand justice and who challenge the impunity of the military and the civil patrols.

On September 3, 1992, Pedro Perez Lopez, an active member of CERJ who has denounced human rights violations since 1988, was chased out of his village by two armed men with masks over their faces. This incident followed a complaint which Mr. Perez filed on August 30, 1992 with the office of the local Ombudsman for Human Rights in Santa Cruz del Quiche. The complaint accused the civil patrollers in his village of having murdered Catarino Chanchavac Larios on August 26, 1992. Today, Mr. Lopez lives in total insecurity and fear. "I practically never leave my house now and I never go to market anymore. The

---

[131] *See the report by Robert Carmack (compiler) "Guatemala, Harvest of Violence," 1991, page 520.*

patrollers are always threatening me and saying that I am a guerrilla. They shoot into the air outside my house at night."[132]

On March 12, 1992, Pedro Marroquin, Sebastian Marroquin and Miguel Cuin Marroquin, from Paxot III, Quiche filed a complaint with the Ombudsman for Human Rights office in Santa Cruz del Quiche. The complaint stated that ex-heads of the civil patrol and past and present military commissioners from their community had accused them of being guerrillas and threatened them with death. On March 24, 1992, the military commissioners and civil patrollers held a public meeting in Paxot. Military commissioner Miguel Leon Yacon informed the people that he and other commissioners and civil patrollers had been called in by the local Ombudsman for Human Rights in Santa Cruz del Quiche to give statements about the alleged persecution. He said that the complaint was a lie and criticized the three men for filing it. The three men filed another complaint on March 25, 1992 about the previous day's events. Sebastian Marroquin Cuin stated that civil patrollers had threatened that they were "going to get him" for filing the complaint.[133]

On April 30, 1991, Marcelina Calel Lopez filed a complaint with the Ombudsman for Human Rights in Santa Cruz about the assassination of her son. "On 19 April 1991, my son, Miguel Calel, was assassinated . . . I had not presented a complaint about the assassination earlier, because I was scared and frightened of what could happen if I did."[134]

(ii). Judges are threatened.

Several judges have received serious threats for pursuing cases of human rights violations perpetrated by civil patrollers. According to the President of the Judiciary, many courts were closed in October 1991 because of the intimidation of the judges.[135] The following cases illustrate the threats against judges who pursue cases involving the civil patrols in rural Guatemala.

In May 1992, 150 armed civil patrollers from San Ildefonso Ixtahuacan, Huehuetenango seized the local prison and demanded the release of their civil patrol leaders, Samuel Domingo, Mario Ramirez, and Juan

---

[132] *Interview by author with Pedro Perez Lopez July 1992, and complaint from Ombudsman for Human Rights, September 1992.*
[133] *Interview by author July 1992.*
[134] *See the petition filed with the local Human Rights Ombudsman in Quiche, April 30, 1991.*
[135] *The President of the Judiciary made this remark during an address on October 4, 1992.*

Lopez Morales, who were charged with murder. The civil patrollers threatened the judge and other employees with death if their leaders were not immediately released. The judge allowed the three accused murderers to leave, because he feared for his life. The Adjunct Ombudsman, Mr. Alvarez Guademuz, had to intervene before two of the 150 civil patrollers involved in this incident were finally arrested.

On March 19, 1992, a judge from Sacapulas, Quiche wore a bulletproof vest during a judicial investigation to Parraxtut to exhume the body of Miguel Tiu Imul in search of forensic evidence for the cause of his death. The judge was afraid that the civil patrollers would violently interfere with the investigation.[136] Miguel's family had accused the civil patrol leaders of murdering him, and the judge had previously imprisoned one of the accused for threats.[137]

Judges who proceed with their work are threatened and intimidated. Other judges, observing the peril of pursuing cases of human rights violations, refrain from investigating such cases and perpetuate the failure of Guatemala's justice system.

(iii). The military, not the police, enforces internal security.

Internal security is enforced by the military rather than the police. The government has not restricted the power of the military, which fully controls internal and external security through the armed forces and the police forces of Guatemala. The military is in charge of the country's internal security apparatus, including the Mobile Military Police (which deal with military matters), the National Police (which deal with civil matters), the Treasury Police (aligned with the military intelligence department), and the civil patrols.

President Serrano has not tried to separate the military and police forces. Under the Serrano administration, the Hunapú Task Force was created, allegedly "to combat common crime." The Hunapú coordinates joint operations between the Military Police, the Treasury Police, the National Police and the Mobile Police. The administration continues to sustain the Hunapú force even though the Hunapú force is accused of assassinating a student, Julio Roberto Cuc Quin, at the student parade *Huelga de Dolores* in March 1992, and of violently destroying several peaceful squatter settlements in Guatemala City in May 1992.

---

[136] *Authors interview with judge on March 19, 1992. For a history of the violence of the civil patrollers in Parraxtut, see the Americas Watch report, "Guatemala: Army Campaign Against Human Rights Activists Intensifies," published in May 1990.*

[137] *The judge detained Juan de Leon Perez from January 7-9, 1992.*

The military command of the police limits independent investigations of human rights abuses and reinforces the impunity of the armed forces. The police are also affected by a lack of training, outdated equipment, and limited authority. Moreover, the police themselves are accused of human rights violations, assassinations, disappearances, and torture.

(iv). The police fail to investigate human rights abuses.

The investigative power of the police in rural Guatemala is restrained as a result of their subordination to military authority and the shortage of policemen. There are only 3,000 civil policemen for the whole country of nine million people, and the police are largely absent from rural Guatemala where the civil patrols exercise police powers. The following cases illustrate that the police curtail criminal investigations and procedure in cases where the civil patrols or military are involved.

> On May 18, 1992 the police in Joyobaj verbally abused Maria Garcia from Tunaja in Zacualpa, Quiche, and they attacked her interpreter. Maria Garcia filed a complaint about the attack with the Justice of Peace in Santa Cruz del Quiche, on May 19, 1992.[138]

> Civil patrol leader Santos Coj Rodriguez was arrested after he was accused of eight murders and illegal burials in Tunaja, Quiche. In early October 1991, he "broke out" of prison, apparently aided by two national police officers. The press reported that the Attorney General had initiated proceedings against the two men involved.[139] In a recent interview, the Attorney General denied that the police was involved at all and exclaimed how easy it was to escape from prison.[140]

The police are further restrained from pursuing investigations into human rights violations because of the repercussions of pursuing perpetrators who are associated with, or are members of, the security forces. This is illustrated by the murder of Merida Escobar, the chief police investigator in the highly publicized assassination of the anthropologist Myrna Mack Chang.

(f). Chunima: a case study of the failure of the administration of justice.

The Chunima case is the only CERJ case to proceed to trial and sentencing stages. This case embodies the failings of the judicial system, including the failure of the *habeas corpus* remedy; the failure to protect witnesses; the failure of the police to arrest alleged perpetrators of human rights violations; the

---

[138] *Testimony taken by RFK delegation in Santa Cruz del Quiche, June 1992.*
[139] *See the report "Escapa inn ex-patrullero civil sindicado de varios crimenes," published by Siglo Veinliuno on October 12, 1991.*
[140] *Interview by author with Attorney General Valladares on August 25, 1992.*

failure of the prosecution and of the conviction. The case also typifies the extent to which members of CERJ have not been able to secure relief for the violations committed against them.

Sebastian Velasquez Mejia was the CERJ delegate in Chunima and an advocate of the abolition of the civil patrols. He had stopped participating in the civil patrols in 1988 and had received numerous death threats from the civil patrol leaders in his town. Sebastian had filed several complaints against Manual Perebal Ajtzalam and other patrol leaders of threatening him and other non-patrollers.

On July 18, 1988, Sebastian and other Chunima residents filed a complaint with the Human Rights Ombudsman about harassment from soldiers and civil patrollers from a neighboring community, Xepol.

On September 12, 1988, a group of residents from Chunima, including Sebastian, filed a complaint with the Ombudsman for Human Rights in Santa Cruz del Quiche of beatings, threats and house searches by soldiers on September 10th.

On September 13, 1988, after a village meeting organized by Sebastian, Chunima residents sent a letter to the Governor of Quiche requesting that the army be removed from Chunima because of the military's abusive behavior against residents.

On September 22, 1988, Sebastian filed a complaint with the Human Rights Ombudsman in Guatemala City, the Congressional Human Rights Commission, President Vinicio Cerezo, and the President of the Supreme Court demanding an investigation into the military's occupation of Chunima on July 27th and threats from soldiers against residents.

On May 26, 1989, Sebastian filed a complaint with the Ombudsman for Human Rights in Quiche about death threats made by civil patrollers, Diego Perebal Ic, Manuel Perebal Atjzalam and Manuel Leon Lares. They had threatened to kill Sebastian and had attempted to abduct two non-patrollers on May 24th. The petition sought the intervention of the Minister of Defense.

On June 5, 1989, the Ombudsman of Quiche summoned Sebastian to ratify his complaint of May 26th, and Sebastian reiterated that Diego Perebal Ic had threatened to cut off his head for encouraging residents to terminate their patrol duty.

The police instituted no investigations and no arrests were made based on these threats.

On October 6, 1990 at 8:00 a.m., Sebastian Velasquez Mejia was kidnapped from the Pan American highway, a few miles from his home, by men in a grey pick-up truck. Approximately fifty people witnessed the kidnapping. According to eyewitnesses in this group of people, Manuel Perebal Atjzalam pointed out Sebastian to the kidnappers. CERJ filed a *habeas corpus* application with the justice of the peace in Santa Cruz del Quiche fifty minutes after the kidnapping. The application demanded an immediate investigation and information about Sebastian's whereabouts. At 7:45 p.m. on the same day, CERJ filed a *habeas corpus* application by telegram with the President of the Supreme Court and the Human Rights Ombudsman in Guatemala City.

On October 8th, the Mutual Support Group ("GAM"), a human rights group of relatives of people who have disappeared, filed another *habeas corpus* application with a court in the Guatemala city.

On the same day, a body carrying Sebastian's identification card was found in Guatemala City. His family, however, was not informed about this discovery until October 18th. The official autopsy report stated that Sebastian was killed by strikes to the thorax and abdomen.

On October 17, the National Police issued a statement to the press saying that Sebastian had not been kidnapped, but that he had gone to the city of his own will and had died of alcohol poisoning. The doctor who performed the autopsy subsequently met with representatives of the human rights organizations Americas Watch and Physicians for Human Rights. He informed them that he had found no signs of intoxication.[141]

On December 8th, a companion of Sebastian's, Jose Velasquez Morales, presented a petition for the exhumation of Sebastian's cadaver. The exhumation took place on December 12th and Sebastian's body was identified.

After Sebastian's abduction, his family and friends fled Chunima. They had also previously received threats and feared for their lives. Five men, Manuel Perebal Morales, Diego Perebal Leon, Jose Suy Mendez, Jose Velasquez Morales and Manuel Suy Perebal, sought refuge in the CERJ office in Santa Cruz del Quiche and others fled to the GAM office in Guatemala City. On October 13, 1990, the five men who sought

---

[141] *See the petition from Americas Watch to the Ambassador of the Inter American Commission on Human Rights on April 4, 1991.*

refuge in Quiche, accompanied by the Adjunct Ombudsman for Human Rights, Alvarez Guademuz, CERJ leaders and soldiers, tried to enter Chunima. The civil patrollers under command of Manuel Perebal Atjzalam aggressively threatened them. One patroller fired shots and others shouted "Open fire!" as they entered the village. The delegation fled. At 11 p.m. that evening CERJ filed a *habeas corpus* application on behalf of the five threatened men.

On October 14th, the five CERJ members filed a *habeas corpus* application for family members who had remained in Chunima. The document expressed their fear for the safety of their relatives, because of the recent attack by civil patrollers. On October 18, 1990 the five men also filed a complaint with the Ombudsman for Human Rights in Quiche about ongoing threats by Manuel Perebal Ajtzalam. They finally returned to Chunima, despite the threats of October 13th, accompanied by Alvarez Guademuz and the Human Rights Ombudsman, Ramiro de Leon Carpio. The office of the Human Rights Ombudsman promised regular visits to ensure their security. No visits were made for three months. The next visit was to investigate the shooting of two of the five men: Diego Perebal Leon and Manuel Perebal Morales.

On October 25, 1990, Rafaela Capir Perez, Sebastian's wife, filed a criminal complaint against Manual Perebal Ajtzalam for the abduction and killing of her husband and demanded his immediate capture. Three of the five refugees, Manuel Perebal Morales, Diego Perebal Leon and Manuel Perebal Ic, were eyewitnesses to the incident and testified in court that Manuel Perebal Atjalam was responsible for Sebastian's kidnapping and murder. As a result of these testimonies, the Quiche district Court Judge, Roberto Lemus Garza, issued a warrant for the arrest of Perebal Ajtzalam on January 21, 1991. The police failed to carry out the arrest. Judge Lemus received constant death threats and consequently fled the country in August 1991.

On February 17, 1991 at 5:30 a.m., two of the eyewitnesses, Diego Perebal Leon and Manuel Perebal Morales, and their father, Juan Perebal Xirum, were shot on the way to the market. Juan and Manuel were killed and Diego was left paralyzed as a result of the shooting. Diego recognized two of the six attackers as civil patrollers, Manuel Perebal Ajtzalam and Manuel Leon Lares. The police had also ignored a warrant for the arrest of Manuel Leon Lares, which was issued in March 1990 after his participation in an attack on a group of human rights advocates.

On February 18th, arrest warrants were issued for the two patrol leaders by the Justice for the Peace in Chichicastenango. Not until April 26, after fifteen members of the U.S. Congress had written to President Serrano expressing concern for the situation in Chunima,[142] did the police attempt their first arrest. Armed patrollers blocked their entrance into the village and the police left. On June 13th, the police again tried to arrest them, but were met with the same response and detained no one. On that day the patrollers temporarily restrained a CERJ member who accompanied the police as their guide.

On July 30, 1991, the Guatemalan Government was called to appear before the Organization of American States ("the OAS") to answer to a complaint about the cases of human rights abuses in Chunima. Only on that day were the men arrested by the police.

In November 1991, a trial began against Manuel Leon Lares and Manuel Perebal Ajtzalam for the murder of Manuel Perebal Morales and Juan Perebal Xirum and for paralyzing Diego Perebal Leon. Manuel Perebal Ajtzalam was also charged with threatening non-patrollers and participating in the kidnapping of Sebastian Velasquez Mejia. Two eyewitnesses identified Manuel Perebal Ajtzalam and Manuel Leon Lares as the murderers of Manuel and Juan. Several residents from Chunima came forward to testify about previous threats, but some were not heard, because the representative from the District Attorney's office failed to turn up. The Adjunct Ombudsman, Alvarez Guademuz, was also listed as a witness about previous threats, but he was never heard. Other witnesses, including staff of the Ombudsman's office and members of camera crews from Guatemala's T.V. Channel 11, who were present at the incident on October 13th, claim that they never received their summonses to testify. The judge refused to allow the screening of video footage filmed during the Ombudsman's visit to Chunima and showing Manuel Perebal Ajtzalam harassing two of the victims, Diego and Manuel. Manuel Perebal Ajtzalam had no alibi and simply denied any involvement in the February 17th killings. On July 15, 1992, the two accused were acquitted on all counts for insufficient evidence. Abduction charges against them were dropped. The sentence is being appealed.[143]

The judge who heard the case also felt intimidated. Judge Juan Francisco Perez Munoz slept at the court house throughout the trial, because he feared that he would be attacked at home. One morning, during the trial, a white car appeared at the courthouse and three armed men got out and asked for him.[144]

---

[142] *See the Human Rights Watch World Report of 1992, page 237.*
[143] *Information collected by the author during 1990-1992.*
[144] *Interview by author with the judge during May 1992.*

Although the OAS issued a specific demand to the Guatemalan Government to protect witnesses and family members of the victims during the period of trial, the only action taken was a visit by the Governor of Quiche to Diego Perebal Leon and his family a couple of days before the OAS demand was up for review in December 1991.

(g). Conclusions.

President Serrano's promise that he would end Guatemala's devastating human rights abuses remains unfulfilled. Although the Government has created certain institutions to monitor human rights in Guatemala, those institutions are largely ineffective and are hampered by a lack of jurisdiction and power to prosecute human rights violators.

President Serrano persists with criticism of human rights advocates and organizations and, in so doing, strengthens the impunity of the military and the civil patrols.

The government allows a vicious campaign of vilification and denigration against CERJ and Amilcar Mendez to continue.

By tolerating forced recruitment into the civil patrols, the Government violates the provisions of the International Labor Conventions.[145] Signatory countries are obliged under Convention 105 "to take effective measures to secure the immediate and complete abolition of forced or compulsory labor as specified by the convention." The Guatemalan government is not taking any steps to abolish the civil patrol system, and encourages and supports the civil patrols.

The Government tolerates the impunity of the military and the civil patrols and the failure of the administration of justice. The civil patrols exert authority in the highlands of Guatemala. Civil patrollers interfere with the judicial process, threaten witnesses and judges, and continue to persecute victims of human rights abuses. Military control over rural Guatemala is reinforced by the civil government's failure to exercise control over internal security. Although adequate mechanisms exist for relief, the government, law enforcement agencies, and the judiciary do not vigorously or properly protect human rights. Government officials often ascribe the existing impunity to inefficiency, corruption and a lack of resources in the judicial system.[146] The Guatemalan Attorney General asserts that the country lacks the infrastructure to ensure the protection of human rights and that the rural areas are practically under martial law and therefore largely impenetrable to civil authorities.[147] In taking these positions, the Guatemalan government attempts to avoid responsibility

---

[145] *Guatemala became a party to Convention No. 105 on December 9, 1959 and to Convention No. 29 on June 13, 1989.*

[146] *Author's interview with Oscar Villar Anleu on August 26, 1992.*

[147] *Delegation interview with Asisclo Valladares on June 12, 1992.*

for human rights abuses and for the prosecution and punishment of human rights violators. The government's attitude reveals the real obstacle to justice in Guatemala: the government's lack of political will to terminate military impunity and to assert civilian authority over the military establishment and the civil patrols.

The U.N. expert on Guatemala, Christian Tomuschat, recommended that military strategy in rural Guatemala be revised profoundly. He added that only one solution was appropriate, namely, to disband and disarm the civilian defense patrols.[148]

---

[148] *See paragraphs 4 and 7 on page 16 of the Tomuschat report about human rights in Guatemala. The report was prepared in accordance with paragraph 11 of Commission Resolution 1991/51, January 21, 1992.*

VII. CONCLUSIONS.

(1). The Civil Patrols

a. The practice of forcing recruits against their will to participate in the civil patrols is pervasive and constitutes a clear and consistent pattern of violation of human rights. The civil patrol recruitment practice abrogates the right of free association and the right not to associate under both the Guatemalan Constitution and International Law.

b. The activities of the civil patrollers violate the international conventions on human and labor rights and the Constitution of Guatemala which guarantee the rights to life, liberty, justice, security, peaceful assembly, freedom of expression and freedom of movement.

c. The civil patrol system discriminates against men from the indigenous communities who are almost exclusively recruited into the civil patrols.

d. Minors are forcibly recruited to participate in the civil patrols, clearly violating the rights of children under the Guatemalan Constitution and International Law.

e. Members of the civil patrols violently respond to opposition and they have assassinated, assaulted, threatened and intimidated non-patrollers and human rights advocates.

f. The civil patrollers act with impunity, supersede the justice system and dominate the indigenous communities in the highlands of Guatemala. They exhort free labor from local men and maintain tight surveillance over the communities. Civil patrollers interfere with the judicial process. Patrollers intimidate and threaten judges, victims and their families, and witnesses to crimes committed by the civil patrollers.

(2). The Military.

a. The military dominates civil society in rural Guatemala. The army employs the civil patrols as a counter-insurgency force, to control the population and to eliminate dissent. The civil patrols act as agents of the military. Through persecution by proxy, the military escapes accountability for human rights abuses committed by the civil patrollers and by members of the armed forces.

b. The armed forces are legally and organizationally responsible for the civil patrols. The military provides weapons to the civil patrols and supervises their activities. The military forces participation in the civil patrols and harasses and intimidates non-patrollers.

c. The military attacks human rights organizations and advocates of human rights, notably CERJ members and Amilcar Mendez Urizar.

(3). The Civil Government.

a. The Guatemalan government fails to protect human rights. The government neglects its constitutional obligations to the citizens of Guatemala and does not fulfill its duties under international human rights and labor laws.

b. President Serrano has labeled human rights advocate Amilcar Mendez as a collaborator of the insurgency. President Serrano's unwarranted remarks seriously threaten the safety of Mr. Mendez and invite further attacks against human rights advocates.

c. The government appears determined to maintain the civil patrol system, despite the appalling human rights record of the civil patrols. The government allows the military to perform internal security functions and fails to sustain and develop an autonomous police force to uphold the law and to investigate human rights violations. The government tolerates serious human rights violations committed by the military, paramilitary groups and by civil patrols against human rights activists, non-patrollers and residents of rural Guatemala. The government encourages human rights abuses, because it fails to enforce the rule of law and to end the impunity of the military and the civil patrols.

d. The Guatemalan judicial system is flawed and the judiciary fails to protect human rights and to provide redress for victims of human rights abuses.

VIII. RECOMMENDATIONS.[149]

(1). THE GUATEMALAN GOVERNMENT.

a. The Guatemalan government should vigorously protect the human rights of all citizens as required under international laws and the Guatemalan Constitution. The international human rights covenants, to which Guatemala is a signatory, require parties to respect the rights specified in those treaties and to ensure that everyone in the country enjoys those rights. The Guatemalan government should support state institutions and all the structures through which public power is exercised to ensure the free and full enjoyment of rights by all Guatemalans.

b. The government should abolish the civil patrols. In the interim, the civil patrols should be immediately disarmed. The government should renounce forced participation in the civil patrols and bring violators to justice.

c. The government should ensure that the military end its attacks against non-patrollers, members of CERJ, Amilcar Mendez, human rights advocates and citizens. The government should provide public support and active protection to human rights organizations.

d. The government and military leaders should condemn human rights abuses by civil patrollers, soldiers, paramilitary groups and military officers. President Serrano, his government and leaders of the security forces should openly promote respect for human rights.

e. President Serrano should repudiate his public statements linking Amilcar Mendez to guerrilla groups.

f. The government should assert strong civilian authority over the military forces. Military officers must be subject to the same laws, procedures, and other constitutional standards as all citizens. Members of the security forces and the civil patrols should be instructed that they have a duty not to obey orders which will result in the violation of human rights. Obstruction of investigations about human rights violations should not be tolerated and should immediately be prosecuted. Allegations against members of the military and the civil patrols about human rights violations should be investigated by an independent police force, defendants should be tried by independent tribunals in accordance with international standards of due process, and those found guilty should be punished. Military courts should not have jurisdiction over human rights violations.

---

[149] *See Amnesty International report "Human Rights Violations Against Indigenous Peoples," pp 102-112.*

g. Civil institutions should ensure strict control over all officials responsible for arrest, detention, and imprisonment. Only authorized officials should be allowed to carry out arrests.

h. The government should uphold the rule of law. The civil government should assertively prevent, investigate, and punish any violation of the rights recognized by the Constitution and the international human rights and labor treaties to which Guatemala is a signatory. Such cases include the unsolved deaths of CERJ members and non-patrollers and all other complaints about human rights violations documented in this report.

i. The ties between the military and the national police make the police dependent on the military and organizationally part of military mechanisms. The government should initiate reforms which would establish and promote an independent, civilian, professional police force. The police should be strengthened and allowed to perform internal security functions independently from military authority.

j. The Guatemalan government and the judiciary should prosecute the physical perpetrators of attacks, and also those who may have directed, sanctioned, or ordered such abuses.

k. The civilian government should politically empower the judiciary in addition to providing technical assistance. To this end, the government should take active steps to curb military power and the dominance of the civil patrols over the indigenous communities in rural Guatemala. Fair and equitable judicial procedures should be instituted and enforced to protect the victims of human rights violations. The government should provide adequate protection to the victims and witnesses of human rights violations. The Guatemalan government should continue to pursue legal and judicial reform to attempt to restore the rights violated and to provide compensation as warranted for damages resulting from the violations. The Guatemalan Congress should rapidly enact codes of legal, military and criminal procedure to ensure that constitutional rights are promoted and protected.

l. The government should strengthen the mandates of the three government institutions responsible for investigating human rights violations. Adequate funds and resources should be made available to human rights monitoring groups. Members of non-governmental and human rights organizations should be appointed to the three governmental human rights organizations in order to strengthen their autonomy. The office of the Ombudsman for Human Rights should be allowed to prosecute violators of human rights.

m. The government should establish effective mechanisms to specifically identify human rights abuses against indigenous people. In this regard, the government should apply the Guatemalan Constitution to ensure that authorities at all levels protect the indigenous communities against such abuses.

n. Legal proceedings involving members of the indigenous communities should always be conducted in their own language or proper interpretation services should be provided.

o. The government should ensure that justice is equally available to all people living in Guatemala, regardless of their origin and the isolated areas in which they live.

p. The government should recognize discrimination against members of the indigenous communities as a key element of human rights violations committed by the civil patrols, military, and civil authorities. The Guatemalan government should support efforts of the United Nations working groups on Indigenous Populations to promote the protection of the human rights of indigenous peoples.

q. An independent commission should be appointed to impartially investigate allegations of discrimination, to ascertain the extent of discrimination against indigenous peoples, and to make recommendations. The Commission should also examine whether the Guatemalan Constitution has been fully applied to ensure the protection of the rights of the indigenous people, and identify the reasons for obstructing Constitutional guarantees of the rights of the indigenous communities. Non-governmental organizations working with members of the communities and representatives from the communities should actively participate in the commission and the inquiry.

r. The government should make human rights education material available to the indigenous communities in indigenous languages and ensure that they know how to seek remedies if their rights are violated. Victims of abuses, or their families in instances of disappearances or extrajudicial executions, should be compensated for the abuses they have suffered. Compensation should include medical treatment and rehabilitation where required and financial compensation commensurate with the abuses inflicted.

(2). THE U.S. GOVERNMENT.

a. The U.S. should call upon the Guatemalan government to abolish and disarm the civil patrols.

b. The U.S. government should continue to enforce the provisions of the 1993 Foreign Assistance Act which tie aid to improvements in human rights. Specifically:

  (i). The Congress should impose a moratorium on foreign military financing assistance and require that all economic support funds to Guatemala be used solely by civilian and non-governmental agencies.

  (ii). The Committee on Appropriations should continue to subject all aid to Guatemala to regular notification procedures. Such aid should also remain subject to measurable progress by the Guatemalan government to improve its human rights record and to alleviate persistent concerns about the human rights situation in Guatemala and the human rights violations perpetrated by members of the military and the civil patrols.

  (iii). The Congress should ensure that the Guatemalan government submit a report by May 1, 1993, describing the actions of the Guatemalan government to investigate and bring to justice those responsible for human rights murders, disappearances, and other violations including information about the government's investigations and prosecution of those responsible for the murder of Myrna Mack; the murder and abduction of Hector Oqueli and Gilda Flores; the massacre of villagers at Santiago Atitlan; and the kidnapping and murder of CERJ members Sebastian Velasquez Mejia, Juan Perebal Xirum and Manuel Perebal Morales.

  (iv). The relevant committees should continue to take into consideration the extent to which the Guatemalan government has acted vigorously to solve cases of human rights abuses, in particular those related to members of CERJ.

  (v). The U.S. government should continue to consult with the appropriate human rights and congressional committees prior to any proposed sales of military equipment, government or commercial aids funds to Guatemala.

  (vi). Congress should prohibit any "non-lethal" and "lethal" aid and commercial sales of military equipment to Guatemala, until significant and measurable improvements have been made in safeguarding human rights, prosecuting perpetrators of human rights abuses, and until the armed conflict has been peacefully resolved through a negotiated settlement. The transfer of aircraft from the Department of Defense to the Drug Enforcement Administration for activities in Guatemala must remain prohibited.

(vii). Funds to monitor a peace agreement and for retraining, relocating, and re-employing former combatants and non-combatants in civilian occupations affected by the conflict should be disbursed only after the Guatemalan government and the URNG have signed a lasting peace agreement and the civil patrols have been disbanded.

(viii). No funds in the Foreign Assistance Act should be obligated or extended to provide any assistance for any project or activity which contributes to the violation of internationally recognized workers' rights, as defined in section 502 (a) (4) of the Trade Act of 1974 and of workers' rights in Guatemala.

(ix). The Committee on Appropriations should continue to monitor efforts by the Guatemalan Supreme Court to modernize the criminal justice system. The U.S. government should specifically monitor progress by the President of the Supreme Court to introduce and sustain greater oversight of lower court judges to combat corruption and to ensure fair application of the law; to create a criminal investigation capacity under the authority of the courts instead of the National Police or the military; to establish municipal courts and forensic medical facilities in each of the 330 municipalities; to provide training for judges, investigators and prosecutors; and to attend to the most serious unsolved murder cases and cases of human rights violations.

(3). THE INTERNATIONAL COMMUNITY.[150]

a. The U.N. Commission on Human Rights should suspend its Advisory Services Program, mandated under item 19 of the U.N. Commission's agenda, in Guatemala. The Special Expert should be replaced with a permanent Special Rapporteur, mandated under article 12. The U.N. Working Group on Indigenous Populations should actively monitor the human rights violations against the indigenous people of Guatemala.

b. The Inter American Commission on Human Rights of the Organization of American States ("OAS") should consider the cases of human rights violations referred to in this report. On site investigation should be conducted into abuses committed by the civil patrollers and the military. The OAS should ensure that the special circumstances facing the indigenous people of Guatemala and the human rights violations which they endure are adequately addressed in reports about Guatemala. The OAS should consider methods to protect the rights of indigenous people more effectively in

---

[150] See "Crisis Point," page 119.

Guatemala, particularly with regard to the civil patrol system which targets members of the indigenous communities.

c. The Inter American Commission should recommend that the civil patrols be disarmed and abolished.

d. The International Labor Organization ("ILO") should investigate the breaches by the civil patrollers of the ILO Conventions relating to child, forced and free labor in Guatemala. The ILO should condemn violations of international labor standards by the Guatemalan government and the civil patrols. The ILO should recommend that the civil patrols be abolished and disarmed.

e. The international community should urge the Guatemalan government to disarm and abolish the civil patrols and to uphold the rule of law in Guatemala.

f. International human rights organizations should continue to closely monitor the human rights situation in Guatemala and to report any human rights violations.

g. The international community should support existing and aid in the establishment of human rights organizations, monitors and advocates in Guatemala.

Excavation site (August, 1990) of a mass grave in Chontola, Guatemala, where civilians were killed by civil patrollers in the early 1980s.

Photos by Vince Heptig

Civil patrollers marching on Army Day in Guatemala City. The banner reads: "The people and the army united will never be defeated."

Civil patroller in Acul, Guatemala.

Amilcar Mendez Urizar recording testimony of military harassment from peasants who have come to his house in Santa Cruz del Quiche.

One of the many children of families who have sought refuge in the CERJ office from violence in their communities.

Photo by Vince Heptig

Photo by Vince Heptig

Amilcar Mendez Urizar (left) meeting with President Jorge Serrano Elias (right) to discuss human rights violations against CERJ in Guatemala.

Appendix 1:

DEATH THREAT TO POPULAR LEADERS JUNE 1992

Amilcar Mendez
Byron Morales
Armando Sanchez
Rosalina Tuyuc
Ninet Montenegro de Garcia
Juan Mendoza

The last popular communist leaders who will be massacred to death because until they are dead we will not be happy.

Anticommunist Unity.

AMILCAR MENDEZ
BYRON MORALES
ARMANDO SANCHEZ
ROSALINA TUYUC
NINET MONTENEGRO DE GARCIA
JUAN MENDOZA

LOS ULTIMOS COMUNISTAS DIRIGENTES POPULARES
QUE MORIRAN MASACRADOS.

PORQUE HASTA QUE MUERAN SEREMOS FELICES

UNIDAD ANTICOMUNISTA.

Appendix 2:

DEATH THREAT FROM PARAMILITARY GROUP JAGUARS OF JUSTICE TO AMILICAR MENDEZ URIZAR, AUGUST 14, 1991

Amilcar Mendez Urizar, the commanders of Jaguars of Justice have been informed that you are participating with the URNG. That you were a founder of CUC and CERJ which have spilt so much blood of the people of Guatemala especially of the Quiche people. As a warning we inform you that you have ten days to live as your participation with communism commits us to declare you the enemy of freedom, in consequence condemned to death.

For a Guatemala without communism.
J.J.

Received 14/8/91 at 8:00 a.m.

Appendix 3:

ANTI-CERJ FLYER DISTRIBUTED IN SANTA CRUZ DEL QUICHE, OCTOBER 1990

TO THE HONOURABLE PEOPLE OF QUICHE WE MAKE KNOWN

ONE: The group CERJ completed two years of disuniting our people, two years of intrigue between us peasants, is it like this or not Quiche people?

TWO: The President of CERJ is about to leave the country and will go abroad, he achieved two objectives: divide the Quiche people and earn money in exchange for the suffering of our brothers and he will enjoy the money for the rest of his life. What will his collaborators do?

THREE: CERJ is paying killers a salary to assassinate people and later appear defenders; they do this to earn money but this will not be left unpunished, all of the deaths of our brothers we have to recover, earlier or later.

FOUR: Money earned by dividing our people is equal to stolen money, it is sour money, money that you cannot spend with satisfaction, money which you do not enjoy!

FIVE: With or without help, with or without condemnation, will continue to be oppressed and eating beans and tortillas. Continue eating but in peace and united.

SIX: The Lawyers Justo Antonio Perez Medrano and Rogelio Rodas Ramirez were given a warning, one has not fulfilled the request, wait for the response that the chief decides to take from our commanders.

SEVEN: We are not attached to any organization, political party, government, etc., we were born from the necessity to unite our indigenous people, therefore it does not interest us the national or international consequences of our actions, it only interests us to unite our people. The end justifies the means!

For the unity of our indigenous people and because our people expect much of us we will find "Justice!"

"The Indigenous Utatlan Movement."

AL PUEBLO HONRADO DEL QUICHE HACEMOS SABER

UNO: EL GRUPO DE COMUNIDADES ETNICAS RUNUJEL JUNAM, CUMPLIO DOS ANOS DE DESUNIR A NUES TRO PUEBLO, DOS ANOS DE INTRIGA ENTRE NOSOTROS LOS CAMPESINOS; ES ASI O NO PUEBLO QUICHELENSE?

DOS: EL PRESIDENTE DEL CERJ ESTA PHOXIMO A ABANDONAR EL PAIS SE IRA PARA EL EXTERIOR, YA LOGRO DOS OBJECTIVOS: DIVIDIR AL PUEBLO QUICHELENSE Y GANAR DINERO A CAMBIO DEL SUPRIMENTO DE NUESTROS HERMANOS Y EL DISPRUTA DE SU DINERO EL RESTO DE SU VIDA - SUS COLABORADORES QUE HARAN?

TRES: EL CERJ ESTA PAGANDO MATONES A SUELDO PARA ASESINAR GENTE Y DESPUES APARECER COMO DEPENSORES, ESTO LO HACE PARA GAUAR DINERO, PERO ESTO NO QUEDARA INPUNE, TODAS--LAS MUERTES DE NUESTROS HERMANOS LOS TENEMOS QUE COBRAR, TARDE O TEMPRANO.

CUATRO: EL DINERO ROBADO ES IGUAL QUE DINERO GANADO A CAMBIO DE DIVIDIR A NUESTRO PUEBLO, ES DINERO SALADO, DINERO QUE NO SE PUEDE GASTAR CON SATISFACCION; DINERO QUE NO DISFRUTARA!

CINCO: CON AYUDA O SIN AYUDA, CON CONDENA O SIN CONDENA, NUESTRO PUEBLO SEGUIRA OPRIMIDO Y COMIENDO FRIJOL Y TORTILLA QUE LO SIGA COMIENDO PERO EN PAZ Y UNIDO.

SEIS: LOS LICENCIADOS JUSTO ANTONIO PEREZ HEDRANO Y ROGELIO RODAS RAMIREZ, SE LES HIZO UNA ADVERTENCIA, UNO NO HA CUMPLIDO, ESPERE LA RESPUESTA QUE LA JEFATURA DECIDIO LA ACCION A TOMAR POR HUESTROS COMANDOS.

SIETE: NO ESTAMOS LIGADOS A MINGUNA INSTITUCION, PARTIDO POLITICO, GOVIERMO, ETC, NACE--MOS DE LA NECECIDAD DE UNIFICAR A HUDSTRO PUEBLC INDIGENA; POR LO TANTO NO NOS IM PORTA LAS CONSECUENCIAS NACIONALBS O INTERNACIONALES DE NUESTRAS ACCIONES, SOLO-NOS INTERESA UNIR A NUESTRO PUEBLO. EL FIN JUSTIVICA LOS MEDIOS!

POR LA UNION DE NUESTRO PUEBLO INDIGENA Y PORQUE NUESTRO PUEBLO
ESPERA MUCHO DE NOSOTROS HAREMOS--"JUSTICIA!"

"MOVIMIENTO INDIGENA UTATLAN."

Appendix 4:

DEFAMATORY FLYER DISTRIBUTED IN SANTA CRUZ DEL QUICHE, DECEMBER 1991 TO JANUARY/FEBRUARY 1992

Amilcar states: I put my foot in it, I denounced a child as a kidnapper.

The child asks: Dad, what is a kidnapping?

The father replies: Ask Amilcar.

Appendix 5:

DEFAMATORY FLYER DISTRIBUTED IN SANTA CRUZ DEL QUICHE, DECEMBER 1991 TO JANUARY/FEBRUARY 1992

Peasant: Where are you going Amilcar?

Amilcar: To Canada, no way am I going to Chiche. Then I will come back with my complaints. This pays a lot of money.

Appendix 6:

TRAVEL PERMIT ISSUED BY CIVIL PATROLS TO VILLAGERS, AUGUST 17, 1989

The village of Vicalama 17/8/89

To whom it may concern (name) has permission for three days to go to Nebaj and onto (Santa Cruz del) Quiche.

For this we request that the authorities and military protect him.

C.V.D.C. (Voluntary civil defense committee)

Appendix 7:

TRAVEL PERMIT ISSUED BY CIVIL PATROLS TO VILLAGERS, AUGUST 7, 1988

This note is proof that (name) is a member of the civil defense committee in the village La Laguna and he asked permission to go to the village of Vicalama.

Sincerely, civil defense committee of the village La Laguna.

Nebaj, 7 August, 1988.

Por este medio el Señor [NAME] es miembro y Colaborador del Comité de defensa Civil del Cantón La Laguna Solicitó permiso para que pueda dirigirse en la Aldea Vicalama.

Atentamente

Nebaj 7 de Agosto de 1988.

Comité de defenza civil del Canton La Laguna

Appendix 8:

CERJ MEMBERS WHO HAVE BEEN ASSASSINATED OR DISAPPEARED

1. Pedro Pablo Ramas assassinated in Choaquerum, Joyobaj, Quiche on June 25, 1988.
2. Pedro Cumez Perez kidnapped and disappeared in San Antonio Palopo, Solola on September 11, 1988.
3. Marcario Pu Chivalan kidnapped and disappeared on Finca Trinidad, Miramar Patulul, Suchitepequez on April 1, 1989.
4. Luis Ruis Luis kidnapped and disappeared on Finca Trinidad, Miramar Patulul, Suchitepequez on April 1, 1989.
5. Agapito Perez Lucas kidnapped and disappeared Finca Trinidad, Miramar Patulul, Suchitepequez on April 7, 1989.
6. Nicholas Mateo kidnapped and disappeared Finca Trinidad, Miramar Patulul, Suchitepequez on April 7, 1989.
7. Valerio Chijal assassinated in El Agostadero, San Andres Sacabaja on September 2, 1989.
8. Maria Mejia assassinated in Parraxtut, Sacapulas, Quiche on March 17, 1990.
9. Jose Vincente Garcia assassinated in Chutzalic, San Pedro Jocoplias on April 10, 1990.
10. Dominigo Castro Alonzo assassinated in Pasaguey, Joyabaj, Quiche on April 13, 1990.
11. Jose Maria Ixcaya assassinated in Canton La Fe, Pujujil, Solola on May 1, 1990.
12. Pedro Tiu Cac kidnapped and assassinated in Racana, Santa Maria Chiquimula, Totonicapan on July 12, 1990.
13. Samuel de la Cruz Gomez kidnapped and disappeared in Chimatzatz, Zacualpa, Quiche on October 2, 1990.
14. Jose Pedro Tin Chivalan assassinated in Racana Santa Maria Chiquimula, Totonicapan on October 2, 1990.
15. Sebastian Velasquez Mejia kidnapped and assassinated in Chupol, Chichicastenango, Quiche on October 6, 1990.
16. Juan Perabal Xirum assassinated in Chunima, Chichicastenango, Quiche on February 17, 1991.
17. Manuel Perebal Morales assassinated in Chunima, Chichicastenango, Quiche on February 17, 1991.
18. Pablo Ajiataz Chivalan assassinated in Santabal, San Pedro, Jocopilas on March 15, 1991.
19. Manuel Ajiataz Chivalan assassinated in Santabal, San Pedro, Jocopilas on March 15, 1991.
20. Camilo Ajqui Giron assassinated on Portrero Viejo, Zacualpa, Quiche on April 14, 1991.
21. Miguel Calel assassinated in Santabal, San Pedro, Jocopilas on April 19, 1991.
22. Santos Toj Reynoso kidnapped in Guatemala City on May 26, 1991. He was from Cruzche IV, Santa Cruz del Quiche.

23. Tomas Ventura Xon assassinated in Canton Quiejel, Chichicastenango, Quiche on June 24, 1991.
24. Celestino Julaj Vincente assassinated in Canton Quiejel, Chichicastenango, Quiche on June 28, 1991.
25. Esteben Tojin kidnapped and disappeared in Mixco, Guatemala City on March 13, 1992.

Appendix 9:

DEFAMATORY PAMPHLET DISTRIBUTED IN WASHINGTON, D.C., OCTOBER 15, 1991

"MR. AMILCAR MENDEZ, CONVERSING WITH PRESIDENT JORGE SERRANO ELIAS TO RESOLVE THE CASE OF PEREBAL ABSALON TERCERO. SOME POSITIVE STEPS HAD BEEN TAKEN, WHICH MR. AMILCAR MENDEZ ACKNOWLEDGED AND FOR WHICH HE THANKED THE PRESIDENT."

CAPTION: PICTURES, JUNE 4th, 1991.

AMILCAR NEFTALI MENDEZ URIZAR

- JANUARY 1981: HE APPEARS AS A MEMBER OF THE E.G.P. (THE GUERILLA ARMY OF THE POOR), A GUERILLA FACTION.

- SEPTEMBER 1981: HIS WIFE MIRIAM DARDON DE MENDEZ, WAS DENOUNCED FOR WORKING IN THE GUATEMALAN SOCIAL SECURITY INSTITUTE IN QUICHE, SUPPLYING SUBVERSIVES WITH MEDICINE.

- OCTOBER 1983: HE IS KNOWN AS SECRETARY OF ELECTORAL MATTERS OF THE PRO-FORMATION COMMITTEE OF THE "UNITED FRONT OF THE REVOLUTION" PARTY (FUR).

- NOVEMBER 1986: HE IS KNOWN AS A MEMBER OF THE CIVIL SELF-DEFENSE PATROLS IN THE DEPARTMENT OF QUICHE. AT THE SAME TIME HE WAS AGAINST THE OPERATION OF THE "ADOLFO V. HALL" INSTITUTE OF SECONDARY EDUCATION IN SAID DEPARTMENT.

- AUGUST 1988: HE EMERGES AS COORDINATOR FOR THE COUNCIL OF ETHNIC COMMUNITIES "RUNUJEL-JUNAM."

- JANUARY 1989: THE EX-GUERILLA OF THE SUBVERSIVE ORGANIZATION "REVOLUTIONARY ORGANIZATION OF PEOPLE IN ARMS" (OPRA), ANGEL REYES MELGAR, WHO RETURNED TO GUATEMALAN TERRITORY FROM SPAIN, PUBLICLY DENOUNCED AMILCAR MENDEZ FOR BELONGING TO THE SUBVERSIVE FACTION OF THE E.G.P. AND CLAIMED THAT THE LATTER WOULD BE NINETH GARCIA'S SUBSTITUTE IN THE MUTUAL SUPPORT GROUP (GAM).

- MARCH 1990: ACCORDING TO PUBLICATION FOUND ON PAGE 2 OF THE DAILY, "PRENSA LIBRE", AMILCAR MENDEZ LABELLED AS OFFENSIVE AND OUTRAGEOUS THE FACT THAT GUATEMALA HAS NOT BEEN SANCTIONED FOR ITS HUMAN RIGHTS VIOLATIONS IN GENEVA.

- APRIL 1991: AMILCAR MENDEZ MANAGED TO DENOUNCE IN BONN, GERMANY, AN APPARENT ATTEMPT TO KIDNAP HIM.

- JUNE 1991: AMILCAR MENDEZ MET WITH JORGE SERRANO ELIAS, PRESIDENT OF GUATEMALA TO RESOLVE THE CASE OF PEREBAL ABSALON TERCERO. SOME POSITIVE STEPS HAD BEEN TAKEN PREVIOUSLY, WHICH MR. AMILCAR MENDEZ ACKNOWLEDGED AND FOR WHICH HE THANKED THE PRESIDENT.